CIVIL RIGHTS
STRUGGLES
around the
WORLD

WE ARE NOT *BEASTS* OF BURDEN

CESAR CHAVEZ AND THE DELANO GRAPE STRIKE

California, 1965–1970

STUART A. **KALLEN**

 TWENTY-FIRST CENTURY BOOKS ■ MINNEAPOLIS

Twenty-First Century Books
A division of Lerner Publishing Group, Inc.
241 First Avenue North
Minneapolis, MN 55401 U.S.A.

Website address: www.lernerbooks.com

Library of Congress Cataloging-in-Publication Data

Kallen, Stuart A., 1955–
    We are not beasts of burden: Cesar Chavez and the Delano Grape Strike, California 1965–1970 / by
Stuart A. Kallen.
      p.   cm. — (Civil rights struggles around the world)
    Includes bibliographical references and index.
    ISBN 978-0-7613-4608-1 (lib. bdg. : alk. paper)
    1. Grape Strike, Calif., 1965–1970—History. 2. Strikes and lockouts—United States—History. 3. United
States—History—20th century. I. Title.
    HD5306.K35 2011
    331.892'83480979488—dc22   2009017435

Manufactured in the United States of America
1 – CG – 7/15/10

CONTENTS

LAYING DOWN THEIR TOOLS

On the morning of September 8, 1965, more than one thousand Filipino farmworkers laid down their pruning shears, hoes, pesticide sprayers, and other farm tools. As the sun rose over the hills, hundreds of workers on nine ranches walked out of the vineyards located near the California town of Delano, population 12,000. By ten o'clock, small groups of laborers were walking back and forth with strike signs in front of the agricultural packing sheds and cold storage plants that lined the railroad tracks running straight through town. Others picketed in front of the large ranches that had provided employment for skilled grape workers for decades.

The workers, mostly single men in their twenties, wanted something from the wealthy grape growers. They were asking for a raise that would bring their pay up to $1.40 an hour, the wage earned by most other farmworkers in California. At the time, the grape workers were making about 90¢ an hour for the grueling field-work in the hot sun. They were also paid 10¢ per lug, or basket, of grapes they picked. With this system, the workers still averaged less than $1.20 an hour. Although grapes are a labor-intensive crop that requires the attention of skilled hands ten months a year, the growers refused the demands of the farmworkers.

HARD, DIRTY, AND DANGEROUS

The running battles between field-workers and large agribusiness (ranches and farms owned by industries) were a fact of life in California. The laborers were among the poorest people in the state, and they suffered indignities on a daily basis. Workers were forced to live in grower-owned labor camps where there were no basic standards for health, safety, and comfort. An online history of farmworkers provides examples:

> At one farm the boss made the workers all drink from the same cup "a beer can" in the field; at another ranch workers were forced to pay a quarter per cup [of water]. No ranches had portable field toilets. Workers'... housing was strictly segregated by race, and they paid two dollars or more per day for unheated metal shacks—often infested with mosquitoes—with no indoor plumbing or cooking facilities.

While living conditions were bad, field-work was hard, dirty, and dangerous. Workers were not provided any safety equipment when working with deadly pesticides such as DDT. Hundreds were maimed or killed in preventable accidents due to poorly maintained farm equipment. As a result, the average life expectancy of a farmworker was forty-nine years.

Larry D. Itliong was well acquainted with the laborers' plight. He had been working in fields since he arrived from the Philippines at the age of sixteen in 1929. He had been organizing U.S. farmworkers into labor associations since 1959, when he formed the Agricultural Workers Organizing Committee (AWOC). Days before the workers began the 1965 strike, Itliong warned them that they would face a tough time. There were many Mexican laborers crossing the

Larry Itliong speaks at a farmworkers' event in California in the 1960s.

border who would gladly take their jobs because they were extremely poor and desperate for work.

The Filipino strikers were facing permanent unemployment. They could be blacklisted (put on a list that denied them future jobs) after the strike, meaning growers would refuse to rehire men who were considered troublemakers. The workers still wanted to strike, however. They only had one condition. According to Itliong, they said, "We don't want to picket our boss. . . . We've been working for him for ten, fifteen, twenty years. We don't want him to get mad at us." As a compromise, strikers were organized to picket the ranches where they had never worked.

■ ■ ■ ■ EVERY WORKER SHOULD SUPPORT THE STRIKE

When the Filipino grape workers went on strike that September morning, the growers immediately panicked. It was the end of summer, and the ripe grapes were hanging heavy on the vines. If they were not picked, packed, and sent to market, the result would be major financial losses.

The growers were not the only ones surprised by the strike. A young Mexican American named Cesar Chavez had formed the National Farm Workers Association (NFWA) with labor organizer Dolores Huerta a few years earlier. The NFWA had about seventy dollars in its bank account and the services of one volunteer lawyer. When Chavez was asked when the NFWA would be prepared for a big strike, he answered "about 1968."

Despite his apprehension, Chavez decided to join ranks with AWOC. In a break with tradition, Filipinos and Mexican Americans, who were often pitted against each other by ranchers, were working together for equal rights. Offering unconditional support for the strike, Chavez issued a press release around September 10 that read, "Now is when every worker, without regard to race, color or nationality, should support the strike and must under no circumstances work in those ranches that have been struck."

Within a week, thousands of farm laborers around Delano joined the strike. Before the year was out, their local struggle had become

Dolores Huerta *(left)* and Cesar Chavez formed the National Farm Workers Association (NFWA) in 1962.

national news and attracted the support of celebrities, senators, and countless middle-class Americans. Two of the strike leaders, Chavez and Huerta, would become heroes to millions of struggling workers throughout the world. This act of defiance by humble farmworkers eventually led to permanent changes in the farm labor laws that protect U.S. field-workers throughout the country.

CHAPTER 1

DECADES OF **STRIFE**

"[California's] agricultural industry
has been sick for a long time,
and there are few sections of the
country where . . . democracy
has been more remote."

— Eugene Nelson, labor organizer, 1966

In 1937 renowned folksinger Woody Guthrie sang about California as a paradise in the song "Do Re Mi." Guthrie was referring to the warm climate, abundant rivers, and rich soil in California where a wide variety of fruits, grains, and vegetables were grown to feed a hungry nation. Guthrie, though, wrote the song for thousands of desperate farmworkers who were pouring into the state in the midst of the Great Depression, a period of economic downturn in the 1930s. After pointing out that California is a paradise to live in, Guthrie warns farmworkers that it won't be so great, unless they have money ("do re me").

Guthrie's genius centered on the fact that he could capture popular sentiments in simple, humorous songs. And "Do Re Mi" perfectly expressed the story of California's agriculture dating back to the 1870s. While promoters long represented the state as a heavenly place filled with abundant vineyards, fields of lettuce, and orange groves, the farmworkers who made paradise possible often lived lives of grim servitude. And despite the image of California as a place of unlimited possibilities, wealth, and freedom, those who worked the fields were denied basic human rights.

MINING FOR WHEAT
The unique circumstances of California's agricultural history can be traced to

Woody Guthrie in 1937. Guthrie was a prolific songwriter who often wrote songs about social justice.

the gold rush that began in 1849. By the mid-1850s, millions of people were moving to California to seek wealth in the goldfields. Some who failed at mining turned to farming. But many of the later gold seekers worked for large mining companies that had taken over most gold-mining operations. The owners of these failed mining companies were not interested in the small-scale agriculture practiced on family farms in the eastern United States. Instead, they wanted to strike it rich by converting the California countryside into what were called bonanza farms, endless fields that would produce great wealth.

As the number of bonanza farms increased, grains such as wheat, oats, and barley came to be known as the second gold discovery. By the 1880s, in little more than two decades, California farms had become the second-largest producers of grain in the country. The people collecting the riches from the land, though, were not men in overalls and women in bonnets and aprons. Instead, they were some of the richest people in the United States, including newspaper publishers, railroad barons, and bankers who didn't even live on the farms they owned. One unnamed commentator complained about these absent landlords saying, "Large farming is not farming at all. It is mining for wheat. In one point of view, it is a manufacturing business in which . . . grain appears in [train] carloads. Such farming holds the same relation to society as does a manufacturing corporation."

■ CHINESE LABORERS

Like most manufacturing, California farm production was dependent on an abundant supply of cheap labor. This was initially provided by Chinese immigrants. They were a critical part of the economic growth of state agriculture in the closing decades of the nineteenth century.

At least one-quarter million Chinese workers emigrated to California beginning about 1850. In 1866, when the Central Pacific Railroad began building the western link of the First Transcontinental Railroad, about eleven thousand Chinese workers were recruited to blast tunnels, build trestles, and lay countless railroad ties. Thousands of them died while carving the railroad line through the treacherous mountain terrain of California's Sierra Nevada.

After the railroad was finished in 1869, thousands of Chinese laborers went to work in the Central Valley of California. Most of these men had come from the Pearl River Delta region in southern China, where their ancestors had farmed for centuries. Drawing on their agricultural experiences from home, the Chinese laborers used innovative construction techniques to drain ponds and build levees (earth ridges to hold back water). They converted the wetlands of the

CALIFORNIA AND THE CENTRAL VALLEY

Redding
SACRAMENTO VALLEY
Sacramento River
Yuba City
Wheatland
Santa Rosa
Sacramento
Berkeley
Stockton
San Francisco
San Jose
San Joaquin River
Salinas
Salinas River
Fresno
Corcoran
Tulare
Woodville
Porterville
Delano
Richgrove
Bakersfield
Santa Maria
Oxnard
Los Angeles
San Diego

SAN JOAQUIN VALLEY

NEVADA

Miles
0 25 50 75 100
0 50 100 150
Kilometers

SIERRA NEVADA

COAST RANGES

PACIFIC OCEAN

CALIFORNIA

COACHELLA VALLEY
IMPERIAL VALLEY

UNITED STATES
MEXICO

MEXICO
BAJA CALIFORNIA

Central Valley
Mountains
International border
State border
Capital city
City

Chinese workers construct a railroad trestle in California in 1867.

Sacramento-San Joaquin River Delta into rich farm fields. For the strenuous labor of turning tens of thousands of acres of swampland into farmland, the farm owners paid each worker about one dollar per day.

When the work was done, many Chinese people settled in the region, growing fruits and vegetables on small plots of land rented from major landholders. Others worked at canning factories or on large farms owned by white businessmen. By the 1870s, nearly half of all agricultural workers in the Sacramento Valley were of Chinese descent.

"DANGEROUS TO THE WELL-BEING OF THE STATE"

Despite their contribution to the state's growth, Chinese people faced severe racism and violence in California. White workers feared competition from the hardworking foreigners. In 1879 these attitudes prompted politicians to amend the California state constitution to say that Chinese people were "dangerous to the well-being of the State."

The 132,000 people of Chinese ancestry in California were barred from working for white-owned business or on projects authorized by state, county, or municipal governments. The constitution also granted towns and cities "all necessary powers . . . for the removal of Chinese" from within their borders.

Three years later, the U.S. government passed the Chinese Exclusion Act. This law prevented all immigration from China and barred Chinese people already in the United States from becoming naturalized, or granted citizenship. People from China were also barred from attending public schools, forbidden from owning real estate, and prevented from obtaining business licenses or government contracts.

After the passage of the Exclusion Act, there was an increase in racist terrorism. In dozens of incidents, white mobs rampaged through Chinese neighborhoods, burned homes, looted shops, and lynched people. An economic downturn that began in 1890 made problems worse. Jobs were scarce for everyone even white workers. Riots broke out in Central Valley towns, and white workers shot and killed hundreds of immigrant workers. They forcibly loaded survivors onto railcars and shipped them to San Francisco before burning their homes and neighborhoods to the ground.

Writing about the anti-Chinese attitudes in 1893, the *Los Angeles Times* stated: "White men and women who desire to earn a living have for some time been entering into quiet protest against vineyardists and packers employing Chinese in preference to whites." While some Chinese laborers remained in the Central Valley, most left for the Chinatown neighborhoods of large cities. By 1900 almost all Chinese people had been forced from the region where their labor had generated hundreds of millions of dollars for the growers.

■ ■ ■ THE ORCHARD OF THE WORLD

The fierce competition over jobs in the Central Valley can be traced to the transcontinental railroad, which changed the dynamics of agriculture in California. The rails linked Central Valley food producers to millions of consumers in the Midwest and East. Their insatiable demand for fresh fruits and vegetables caused a boom in produce production that was so profitable it surpassed the first gold rush. As one grower exclaimed, "It is possible . . . for [California] to become the orchard of the whole world."

With the Chinese gone, many white unemployed factory workers moved from California cities to the Central Valley. These workers quickly became dissatisfied with the hard work and began organizing unions to demand higher wages and shorter workdays. Fortunately for the growers, large numbers of immigrants were arriving from Japan around the turn of the century. These workers were willing to toil in the fields for thirty-five or forty cents a day, less than half the wages earned by the Chinese.

Unable to compete with the cheaper Japanese workers, white laborers largely returned to jobs in the city. By the early 1900s, the

Japanese workers unload a harvest of fruit in California in the early 1900s.

transformation from Chinese to Japanese agricultural workers was nearly complete. On white-owned berry and vegetable farms, at least 85 percent of the workers were of Japanese descent.

■ ■ ■ "A TRICKY AND CUNNING LOT"

With a near complete control of the labor supply in some areas, the Japanese field-workers formed associations to represent their interests. At first the labor organizations acted as job centers, where workers could go to find employment. Before long, however, leaders began organizing work slowdowns and strikes to demand higher wages and better working conditions. These labor actions took place during harvest seasons, when produce was ripe and growers were vulnerable to labor organization demands.

The successful strikes put more money in the hands of Japanese workers. Some laborers saved their money and went into the farming business themselves, leasing or buying some of the most fertile land in the state. The Japanese growers hired Japanese field-workers exclusively, treating them better and paying higher wages. This drove up the cost of labor for white ranchers, who did not welcome the competition from Japanese farmers.

As the power of the Japanese immigrants increased, white growers expressed regret over losing the Chinese labor force. This was the main topic when the California Fruit Growers met for a convention in 1907. The group released a blunt statement that read:

> The Chinese when they were here were ideal. They were patient, plodding, and uncomplaining in the performance of the most menial service. They submitted to anything, never violating a contract. The Japanese now coming in are a tricky and cunning lot, who break contracts and become quite independent. They are not organized into unions . . . but operate as a union would. One trick is to contract their work at a certain price and then in the rush of the harvest threaten to strike unless wages are raised.

The Japanese field-workers were the first in California to use slowdowns, strikes, and other job actions to obtain better wages. However, the power of the Japanese farmworker movement was limited. The actions of the labor associations took place on a local level, and the groups never organized statewide. Without a state organization, the Japanese had little political power, something that would have protected them from the growing hostility of growers and politicians.

■ ■ ■ CEASING TO BE AN IDEAL LABORER

As early as 1900, labor organizations in San Francisco began agitating against Japanese workers and calling for restrictions on immigration from Japan. They were joined by California grower organizations and editors at the San Francisco Chronicle and Los Angeles Times. Once again, politicians in both houses of the California legislature passed resolutions against immigrants. In 1907 U.S. president Theodore Roosevelt bowed to political pressure and negotiated what was called a gentlemen's agreement with Japan. It was not a formal treaty but an "understanding" in which Japan agreed to severely restrict passports for emigration to the United States.

This agreement limited the growth of the Japanese worker population in the United States. In fact, their numbers were reduced, as thousands of young men returned to Japan to escape discrimination. Large growers remained unhappy with competition from Japanese farmers. Their numbers continued to increase even as the Japanese worker population shrank. As California labor commissioner John MacKenzie put it in 1910: "Japanese ambition is to progress beyond mere servility. . . . The moment this ambition [is] recognized, that moment the Japanese ceases to be an ideal laborer."

Because the Japanese were no longer the ideal low-wage, obedient workers they had once been, large growers used the power of the state to stop their advancement. The ranchers turned to legislators from agricultural districts to write laws that limited farmers based on their ethnic background. The most restrictive of these measures was the Alien

Lands Act of 1913. This law prevented noncitizens from purchasing or owning property. Noncitizens were not permitted to sell or give away land to other noncitizens. In addition, noncitizens could only lease a parcel of land for a period of three consecutive years.

The Alien Lands Act was aimed at all Asians, including people from India, the Philippines, and China, but the law was clearly meant to end competition from Japanese farmers. However, people found ways to bypass the law since it did not force those who already owned land to give it up and it did not apply to American citizens of Japanese heritage—those who were born in the United States. At the time of the bill's passage, most Japanese American citizens were small children. Japanese land buyers simply arranged for land to be sold to their children while they remained in control of the acreage. Although thousands circumvented the Alien Lands Act in this way, the law remained in place until 1952, when it was overturned by the U.S. Supreme Court.

THE WHEATLAND HOP RIOT

The relentless pressure against Japanese farm laborers forced those who could not purchase land to move to urban areas. During this same period, about one million immigrants a year were moving to the United States from Poland, Russia, Germany, Italy, and other European nations. While most white immigrants remained in the East and Midwest, tens of thousands made their way to the West Coast. Most of these people were poor and desperate, making them ideal cheap farmhands. But there were American labor agitators among the European migrant workers, and they were anything but respectful of the needs of agribusiness. This touched off the Wheatland Hop Riot in the summer of 1913.

The incident took place on the Durst Ranch, located in the Sacramento Valley near the California town of Wheatland. The ranch, owned by brothers Ralph and Jonathan Durst, was the largest employer of farmworkers in California. It was a major producer of hop flowers used as a preservative and flavoring agent in beer.

The Dursts engaged in a common hiring practice at the time. They placed want ads in dozens of newspapers throughout Nevada, California, and Oregon. The ads said that three thousand laborers were needed for the hop harvest. Actually, the Dursts needed only fifteen hundred workers. By purposely attracting twice as many workers as were needed, the competition among the workers for jobs drove down wages. Laborers had little bargaining power when other workers were waiting to take their jobs if they were fired.

The ads brought twenty-eight hundred job applicants to the Durst Ranch on the first day of August 1913. The crowd that arrived for the three-week harvest was diverse. The men, women, and children, while mostly white, spoke twenty-seven different languages. And the working conditions that they faced were appalling even by 1913 standards.

Hops grow on vines. The vines grew up on special poles 30 feet (9 meters) high. Before machines took over the harvest in the 1940s, workers had to climb the unsteady poles, pick the hops, and load them into sacks that weighed 100 pounds (45 kilograms) each when full. This work was done on most hop ranches by strong, athletic young men, called high pole men, who were well paid. But the Dursts decided to save money by using common laborers, including women and children, to perform this difficult task. For this they would be paid one dollar per 100-pound (45 kg) sack.

To maximize their profits, the Dursts told workers they should not expect free drinking water while they toiled in the 100°F (37°C) heat. Workers would be charged five cents for a glass for water. They were also required to buy food at the Durst company store, where the prices were high and the quality was low.

The workers at the Durst Ranch lived in camps where there were nine doorless outhouses for more than eighteen hundred people. Raw sewage flowed into the nearby irrigation ditches that provided the only free source of drinking water. Waterborne dysentery, which causes severe intestinal problems, was already rampant at the labor camp, and dozens of workers became violently ill. To prevent people from leaving, the Dursts said they would hold everyone's wages until the harvest was over. Those who left early would go unpaid.

Above: Hop pickers stand next to a ripe field at the Durst Ranch in 1913. *Below:* Hop pickers rest in a harvested field at the Durst Ranch. Unfair and unsafe working conditions there led to violence on the ranch in 1913.

THE WOBBLIES FIGHT INJUSTICE

Desperate workers usually submitted to the demands of powerful growers, but this group of immigrant workers contained close to thirty labor organizers. These people belonged to a union called the Industrial Workers of the World (IWW), commonly known as the Wobblies. The IWW was founded in Chicago in 1905, based on the motto "An injury to one is an injury to all." Most Wobblies were Socialists. They believed that all workers should join together to seize power from bosses, factory owners, ranchers, and others who exploited workers. Some Wobblies were militant anarchists. They urged workers in trade unions to overthrow the government and take control of the nation's wealth for all poor people to share.

On August 2, 1913, Richard "Blackie" Ford, an experienced IWW organizer, helped the hops workers form a grievance committee. This group elected leaders who drew up a list of demands for the Dursts. The laborers wanted $1.25 per 100-pound (45 kg) hop sack, fresh ice water in the fields three times a day, and sanitary toilets. They also demanded that high pole men be rehired.

On August 3, about five hundred hop pickers and thirty IWW members organized a strike. They surrounded Ralph Durst's office and presented their list of demands. Durst agreed to all but the wage increase and then ordered the workers from his property. The strikers refused to leave. Durst pushed out of his office, got in his car, and drove to Wheatland to get help. He contacted his attorney, Edmund Tecumseh Manwell, and Yuba County sheriff George H. Voss, who organized a posse, a group of men who would help him maintain order.

The posse arrived at the ranch yelling and shooting their pistols into the air. A shoving match broke out between posse members and the strikers. Guns were drawn, and Manwell was shot dead by a Puerto Rican picker, who was then killed by Durst. The deputies then began firing wildly into the crowd until they ran out of ammunition.

By the time the conflict ended, four people were dead, including an innocent bystander. The sheriff and several strikers were critically injured. Most of the strikers left the scene immediately, but Blackie Ford was eventually captured. Although Ford had advised workers to act in

Members of the Industrial Workers of the World (IWW) union are nicknamed Wobblies. According to author Mark Leier, the term came from an IWW supporter who had not yet mastered the English language:

> The word "Wobbly" . . . humorously illustrates the union's efforts to combat racism. A Chinese restaurant keeper in Vancouver in 1911 supported the union and would extend credit to members. Unable to pronounce the letter W, he would ask if a man was in the "I Wobble Wobble." Local members jokingly referred to themselves as part of the "I Wobbly Wobbly," and by the time of the Wheatland strike of 1913, "Wobbly" had become a permanent name for workers who carried the red [union] card. Mortimer Downing, a Wobbly who first explained the history of the word, noted that the nickname "hints of a fine, practical internationalism, a human brotherhood based on a community of interests and of understanding."

a nonviolent manner, he was blamed for the incident. As a coroner investigating the killings wrote, the deaths occurred at the hands of "rioters incited to murderous anger by I.W.W. leaders and agitators." Ford was tried and convicted of murder in January 1914 and remained in prison for eleven years.

In the aftermath of the Wheatland Hop Riot, growers waged a war against the IWW. Hundreds of private detectives working for the Burns Agency fanned out across the West. They arrested hundreds of hop pickers and Wobblies. Some were beaten, tortured, or bribed into signing confessions that would allow police to arrest Wobblies leaders on trumped-up charges. Commenting on these activities twenty years later, progressive journalist Carey McWilliams described the period as "one of the most amazing reigns of terror that California has ever witnessed."

■ A SATISFACTORY WORKER

Problems with white workers ended in 1917 when the United States entered World War I (1914–1918). Millions of young men were drafted into the armed forces. To prevent labor shortages, California growers began recruiting in Mexico, where millions of impoverished farmers were eager to work in the north. By 1930, 368,000 Mexican field hands were working in California, a number that represented about 75 percent of the state's workforce.

Unlike the Japanese and European laborers who were U.S. residents, most Mexican workers were only in the country temporarily during the growing seasons. This was seen as beneficial to both the growers and the state. The laborers would enter the country, work for low wages, and go home in the winter.

U.S. growers considered the Mexicans perfect workers. As G. P. Clements, manager of the agricultural department

A migrant Mexican worker picks tomatoes in California in the 1930s. Agricultural workers began to come to California for jobs during World War I.

of the Los Angeles Chamber of Commerce, wrote, "No laborer that has ever come to the United States is more satisfactory.... He is the result of years of servitude, has always looked upon his employer as his patron [benefactor], and himself as part of the establishment."

As they had done for generations, the growers used their collective power to keep tight control over their new labor supply. If workers threatened to organize or go on strike, growers threatened them with deportation. By 1924 the owners could make use of the newly created border patrol, which was founded that year. When there was an ample supply of workers, the growers used their political connections to restrict immigration at the border.

■ ■ ■ A MIXTURE OF LABORERS

Despite the influx of Mexicans, there was a scarcity of labor in 1924 as the agricultural business continued to expand in the state. To resolve the problem, the ranchers recruited a large number of Filipino laborers in Hawaii to work in California. Once again, they saw these new arrivals as highly desirable laborers willing to work even harder and for lower wages than those before them. The Filipinos were employed at what was called "stoop work," bending over to tend the crops in asparagus, lettuce, berry, tomato, and grape fields. And accustomed to tropical climates, Filipinos were not averse to working in the rain or in wet, muddy fields.

Because they spoke their native Tagalog language instead of the Spanish of the Mexican workers, growers believed Filipinos would find it difficult to organize mass strikes with other ethnic workers. And the Filipinos worked for wages so low that they undercut the Mexican laborers. This quickly caused animosity between the two ethnic groups. All this was to the advantage of agribusiness interests, as the California Department of Industrial Relations explained in 1930:

> [The] growers prefer to have ... a mixture of laborers of various races, speaking diverse languages and not accustomed

Filipino farmworkers cut lettuce in the 1930s. Filipinos were among the first to organize for better working conditions for farmworkers.

to mingling with each other. The practice is intended to avoid labor trouble which might result from having a homogenous group of laborers of the same race or nationality. Laborers speaking different languages and accustomed to diverse standards of living and habits are not as likely to arrive at a mutual understanding which would lead to strikes or other labor troubles during harvesting seasons, when work interruptions would result in serious financial losses to the growers.

The Filipino workers had little bargaining power during the 1930s, when the Great Depression gripped the United States. With one-third of American adults unemployed, thousands of white laborers were pouring into California seeking work in the fields. Philip Vera Cruz, a Filipino activist who later took part in the Delano grape strike, described conditions his family faced in the vineyards during the 1930s. "[In] the pruning season a grower required new employees to get to the labor camp for two or three days . . . for training without pay. In the training and practice period, those new help were charged 75 cents for board a day. . . . Then after those recruits learned the job, they were paid 10 to 15 cents an hour."

These conditions created an atmosphere of anger among the mainly young, male Filipino workforce, and some began to rebel. In 1933 worker Rufo Canete and other Filipino labor leaders formed the Filipino Labor Union (FLU). The group laid out a list of demands that included raising the minimum wage to thirty-five cents per hour and limiting workdays to eight hours. In addition, the FLU demanded growers eliminate racial discrimination and recognize the union as a bargaining agent for farmworkers.

The FLU set out to recruit workers of all nationalities. It quickly grew to seven chapters with two thousand members. The first union action took place during the harvest of 1934. Leaders called a strike in the Salinas lettuce fields, where 80 percent of the workers were Filipino. Seven thousand workers walked off the job and shut down the lettuce industry. The lettuce growers quickly gave in to FLU demands.

After the harvest, growers throughout the region retaliated. They sponsored vigilante committees made up of off-duty law enforcement personnel, private detectives, and local thugs. These groups operated outside the law to enforce agribusiness interests. They beat, kidnapped, and killed labor leaders. These vigilantes started riots and burned Filipino houses and businesses. Vera Cruz described how

Philip Vera Cruz was a Filipino union activist.

this affected people in Delano: "Filipinos were harassed and driven from their jobs. But the sad thing was they didn't have anywhere else to go. They were pushed to the wall and the whole town was against them. . . . Those poor unwanted people risked their lives even just to go and buy their groceries. In those race riots staged in their camps, some were hurt and one was shot in the head." Despite the terrorism, Filipino unions continued to wage strikes throughout the 1930s.

JAPANESE INTERNMENT

Japanese immigrants faced severe discrimination in California. The situation for Japanese Americans grew much worse at the outbreak of World War II in 1939. The United States declared war after the Japanese air force bombed U.S. ships in Pearl Harbor, Hawaii. Several months later, in February 1942, all persons of Japanese heritage on the West Coast, including U.S. citizens, were rounded up—by government order—and sent to internment camps. The bleak camps consisted of hastily constructed tar paper barracks surrounded by barbed wire. They were located in remote places such as Gila Bend, Arizona; Granada, Colorado; Minidoka, Idaho; and Manzanar, California.

The mass evacuation of more than 120,000 people was strongly supported by white agricultural organizations such as the Western Growers Protective Association, the Associated Farmers, and the California Farm Bureau. Although the Japanese and Japanese Americans were freed after the war ended in 1945, they lost everything—their homes, possessions, farms, and other lands. At the time, it was estimated that the land alone was worth more than half a billion dollars.

THE BRACEROS

The United States entered World War II (1939–1945) in late 1941, and nearly every young, able-bodied American male joined the military in the years that followed. Once again, agribusiness interests were faced with a labor shortage. To alleviate the problem, the U.S. Immigration and Naturalization Service (INS) set up the bracero program to import farmhands from Mexico.

The Japanese removal, advocated by the big growers, cemented the power of the white landowners in the California countryside. It was not until 1988 that Congress passed a bill apologizing to the Japanese for the injustices they suffered during the wartime hysteria. About sixty thousand surviving former prisoners were granted twenty thousand dollars each as compensation for their losses, but the money was not made available until 1993.

This Japanese family awaits relocation in 1942. Families were tagged and moved to internment camps in trucks.

The bracero program was unusual in that it was quietly launched without any public discussion or congressional debate. It was simply set up by an informal agreement between Mexico and the United States. The Mexican government acted as a representative of the workers, while the U.S. government represented the farm employers. The agreement established that braceros would be paid a minimum wage of thirty cents an hour. Farmers would pay the INS for transporting workers to and from Mexico.

The bracero program quickly grew into the largest foreign-worker program in U.S. history. By 1945 about 215,000 Mexican nationals had been employed under the program. Most of the workers were uneducated and from the poorest and most remote regions of Mexico.

Because braceros provided an endless supply of cheap labor, both the U.S. government and the growers considered the program to be an ideal system. However, many braceros did not leave when the work ended. They stayed illegally in the United States, where they married and raised families. By the late 1940s, illegal immigration began to soar along the southern border because of the U.S. government's lax oversight of the bracero program. By 1950 at least one hundred thousand illegal immigrants were working in the fields, according to estimates, while only twenty thousand worked legally through the bracero program.

"The term *bracero* comes from
the Spanish word for arm, *brazos*,
and can be translated loosely in this context
as 'farmhand.' Its literal meaning 'arm-man,'
hints at the function these braceros were to play
in the agricultural economy, supplying
a pair of arms and imposing few obligations
on the host society as human beings."

—Kitty *Calavita*, Inside the State, 1992

Braceros cross an international bridge from the United States to Mexico in 1949. While many braceros returned to Mexico after the harvest each year, many remained illegally in the United States.

To deal with the situation, the INS simply legalized, or "paroled," any workers already in the United States. At that time, Mexicans were referred to as "wetbacks," because many of them swam across the Rio Grande to enter the United States. Within the INS, the process of paroling the illegal immigrants was known as "drying out the wetbacks." When news of the drying-out policy got back to Mexico, it encouraged even more people to illegally immigrate to the United States.

The bracero program operated at a time of amazing growth for California agribusiness. The bonanza in the fields had tripled from $485 million in 1940 to an astounding $1.4 billion in 1945. Growth continued throughout the 1950s. Even through this unprecedented expansion, however, Mexican, Mexican American, and Filipino field hands remained the poorest, worst-treated workers in the United States. Even as the United States grew to be the richest, most powerful nation on Earth, conditions in the fields of California remained unchanged. They were little different from those experienced by Chinese workers in the 1870s.

CHAPTER 2

CESAR CHAVEZ
EMPOWERS THE PEOPLE

We thought that always you had to suffer and be hungry. . . . That was our life."

—Cesar Chavez, recalling his childhood, ca. 1977

When the Delano grape strike began in 1965, community activist Cesar Chavez quickly became the movement's most important leader. His uncommon vigor, intelligence, and leadership ability helped the strike succeed against all odds. To understand how one man proved to be so important to a mass movement, it is necessary to examine the trials and troubles that forged Chavez's personality and provided him with the strength to lead.

Cesar Estrada Chavez was born on March 31, 1927, but his family did not live as migrant workers without homes or hope. They were lucky enough to reside on a farm in the North Gila Valley, along the Colorado River near Yuma, Arizona. Because of the farm's bounty, Cesar's parents, Librado and Juana, always had more than enough vegetables, eggs, milk, and chicken for their family. The Chavezes also owned a small grocery store, auto repair shop, pool hall, and candy counter. They often sold goods to migrant workers and were well aware of the problems the workers faced. When the migrants were hungry and out of money, Juana fed them. Throughout his life,

This photograph, taken in the 1960s, shows the ruins of the Chavez home in the North Gila Valley in Arizona.

Cesar would always remember the generosity his mother showed to the downtrodden.

Chavez's mother also taught him the importance of nonviolence. This was a hard lesson for the boy, who often faced prejudice and discrimination in school. Chavez spoke his native Spanish at home, but Arizona schools required all students to speak English only. Boys and girls who were heard speaking their native language were paddled with a two-by-four by the principal. Offenders were also subjected to public humiliation. On one occasion when Chavez was caught speaking Spanish, his teacher made him wear a sign that said "I am a clown; I speak Spanish." Worse were the taunts from the white children, who hurled racial insults at their Mexican American classmates. These taunts often resulted in fistfights among the students. But Chavez remembered the words of his mother who said, "God gave you senses, like your eyes and mind and tongue, so that you can get out of anything." This inspired Chavez to battle his tormenters with words not fists.

"NAILED TO A CROSS"

It is not surprising that Chavez hated school and preferred to spend his days quietly doing chores on the family farm. However, his idyllic home life began to change during the mid-1930s, when one of the worst droughts in history parched the lands in the western United States. The irrigation canals that the family depended on for water dried up. They scraped by on what little food they could grow, but they were unable to pay the farm's annual property tax bill. By 1937 the tax bill was so large that the county evicted the Chavezes from their land for nonpayment.

Like thousands of other dispossessed Americans during the Depression, the Chavez family loaded up a few possessions in their old car, leaving everything else behind. They headed to the "promised land" of California to start anew, arriving in the Central Valley with forty dollars and nowhere to live. The only work to be found involved picking crops by hand in the hot sun. But even these jobs were scarce, with hundreds of people competing for a few openings. When work was available, wages were less than two dollars a day per worker. This meant that Cesar and all four of his brothers and sisters had to help their parents pick crops from sunup to sundown. Chavez described the arduous nature of the work:

> [Picking lettuce is] just like being nailed to a cross. You have to walk twisted, as you're stooping over, facing the row, and walking [at a right angle] to it. You are always trying to find the best position because you can't walk completely sideways, it's too difficult, and if you turn the other way, you can't [pick]. . . . Many [other] things in farm labor are terrible, like going under the [grape] vines that are sprayed with . . . pesticides. You have to touch those leaves and inhale that poison. Then there are heat and short-handle hoes and stooping over. So many jobs require stooping. . . . All that stooping is why farm workers die before they're fifty.

When there was no work, the Chavezes lived out of their dilapidated car, a 1927 Studebaker. In winter the family lived in makeshift campgrounds with other laid-off workers. With his family constantly on the move, Chavez attended sixty-five separate elementary schools. By eighth grade, fed up with prejudice and mistreatment, he dropped out of school to become a full-time field-worker.

Cesar Chavez in 1942. This portrait was taken for his eighth-grade graduation. It was his final year of formal schooling.

■ LEARNING FROM GANDHI

In 1942 Chavez met and fell in love with a young woman named Helen Fabela while working in a vineyard near San Jose, California. Their romance was put on hold when Chavez joined the U.S. navy. In 1946, when his tour of duty was finished, Chavez returned home and two years later married Helen. The couple settled in San Jose and started a family. Although he was a veteran, Chavez's lack of a high school diploma prevented him from getting a good job. The only work he could find was picking string beans for one dollar a day. With little money coming in, the Chavez family lived in a neighborhood, or barrio, so unpleasant that it was known as Sal Si Puedes, Spanish for "get out if you can."

While working to support his family, Chavez became friendly with a Roman Catholic priest named Donald McDonnell. He had come to Sal Si Puedes to form a congregation. Chavez worked to help McDonnell fix up a small building to hold worship services, and the two men became friends.

McDonnell was more than a priest. He was also a political activist who worked to improve the living conditions of local farmworkers. In long talks with Chavez, McDonnell spoke about the nonviolent teachings of Mohandas Gandhi. This revered leader helped India gain independence from Great Britain in the 1930s and 1940s. Gandhi, who was assassinated in 1948, believed in self-sacrifice to achieve a higher good for his people. For example, although he was quite famous during the 1940s, Gandhi took a vow of poverty, wore little more than a loincloth, and conducted several hunger strikes to draw attention to his cause. As Chavez recalls:

> [Gandhi] prepared himself for [his political causes] by his diet, starving his body so that his spirit could overtake it, controlling the palate . . . then using all his energies to do nothing but service. He was very tough with himself.

Although he was just learning about political activism, Chavez came to understand that he needed to set an example if he wanted

Mohandas Gandhi *(center)* lived simply and dedicated his life to helping India gain independence from Great Britain. This photo was taken during a 1947 hunger strike. Cesar Chavez was greatly influenced by Gandhi's example of nonviolence.

others to follow. By sacrificing for the greater good and living a life of nonviolence, he felt he could become a powerful force to help his people.

■ ■ ■ "I COULD REALLY FEEL IT"

While Gandhi provided a spiritual foundation, the twenty-five-year-old Chavez needed lessons in political organization. These began in 1952, when Chavez attended a community meeting held by activist Fred Ross. Ross, who was forty-two at the time, had been fighting for the rights of migrant workers since the Great Depression. As founder of the Community Service Organization (CSO), he was visiting the barrio to register Mexican American farmworkers to vote so they could elect sympathetic politicians.

Ross had spent about three weeks trying unsuccessfully to find someone who could direct his voter registration campaign. Father McDonnell told him about Chavez, and Ross knocked on his door on a hot June afternoon. At first Chavez was suspicious of this older white man trying to organize Mexican Americans. But Ross had an impressive understanding of the problems in the barrio. He spoke about the polluted creeks and overflowing cesspools running through the neighborhood, which were the source of sores and blisters on the legs of local children. Ross criticized local politicians for allowing this situation to continue. He convinced Chavez that people in the neighborhood could change things by voting. Chavez later recalled, "Fred did such a good job of explaining how poor people could build power that I could even taste it. I could really feel it. I thought, gee, it's like digging a hole. There's nothing complicated about it."

Ross was equally impressed with Chavez, writing in his journal after their first meeting, "Chavez has real push. Understanding. Loyalty and Enthusiasm. Grassroots leadership quality." Ross hired him to head the CSO voter registration project in San Jose. Pay was thirty dollars a week, a huge sum for Chavez, who at that time was working in a local lumberyard for less than half that amount.

■ A RECKLESS ACCUSATION

While registering voters was better than hauling lumber, it was just as difficult in some ways. Most of the people Chavez wanted to register tended to vote for Democratic politicians. This challenged the power of conservative Republicans, who had a lock on the electoral process in California's agricultural districts. To resist the CSO's efforts, local Republican deputy registrars, who supervised voting registration, created barriers for Chavez. He was told he could not speak Spanish while he worked to register people, even though it was the native language of most prospective voters. In addition, the work could only be conducted during daylight hours, when nearly everyone was at work.

Members of the Community Service Organization pose for a photograph in the 1950s. Fred Ross *(front row center)* encouraged Cesar Chavez *(front row, second from right)* and Helen Chavez *(back, third from right)* to join the organization.

Despite the restrictions, Chavez threw himself into the work with a sense of great urgency. He circulated a petition to the state attorney general protesting the intimidation techniques used by county registrars. And with the help of many friends from the barrio, the CSO registered six thousand new voters around San Jose.

Seeing that their antiregistration tactics were failing, the Republicans began falsely claiming that the Mexican Americans were registering illegal immigrants and dead people. They also told newspaper reporters that Chavez was a Communist. This was an era when the United States and the Communist government of the Soviet Union (Russia and fourteen other republics) were engaged a period of intense rivalry known as the Cold War (1945–1991). Communists believe in government control and distribution of production and wealth. There were widespread fears in the United States that Communists would take over the world. Therefore, calling someone a Communist was like calling someone a terrorist. While very few actual Communists were living in the United States, the reckless accusation was commonly used by politicians hoping to make headlines.

In San Jose, conservative white voters feared that Communists were using Chavez and others to promote revolution among the poor. Several people even filed complaints with the Federal Bureau of Investigation (FBI), which sent agents to interview Chavez to determine the threat he posed to the public order. The scheme backfired when the FBI held a meeting with Chavez and Republican officials. After the agents understood the situation, they warned the politicians that their antiregistration tactics were illegal. However, the smear campaign had lingering effects, and some continued to associate Chavez with Communism for decades.

■ ■ ■ ■ "IT WAS ROUGH"

After the incident with the FBI, some residents of the barrio were afraid to associate with Chavez. They feared they might lose their jobs or get evicted from their homes. Others, however, came to respect him as a high-profile community leader, a role Chavez was pleased to assume.

In 1953 he set up a service center for the CSO. People could go there to file complaints about their daily problems with bosses, landlords, dishonest salespeople, and the police. Chavez also spent a great deal of time helping immigrants to become U.S. citizens. Some of those he worked with had been living in the United States more than fifty years, but no one ever taught them how to apply for citizenship. Even in his off-hours, Chavez continued to give to his community. Residents remember how he would buy dozens of tamales, a food made of cornmeal with a meat or vegetable filling, and walk through Sal Si Puedes handing them out to hungry children.

Chavez was willing to spend long hours helping those in need. But he expected them to return the favor by giving small cash donations to the CSO, helping with food drives, and signing petitions. During this period, Chavez learned, "Once you help people, they become very loyal. The people who helped us . . . when we needed volunteers were people we had helped."

Soon Ross promoted Chavez to the position of statewide organizer. With a salary of fifty-eight dollars a week, Chavez began traveling to small towns in the San Joaquin Valley. He held house meetings, signed up new members to the CSO, and organized voter registration drives. While he was eager to challenge the power of politicians and agribusiness interests, the new job required Chavez to move every two or three months. This was extremely hard on Helen Chavez and their family. In 1953 the couple had five children, and three more would be born before the end of 1958. However, Helen supported her husband's work despite the burdens it imposed. As Chavez recalls, "It was rough in those early years. Helen was having babies and I was not there when she was at the hospital. But if you haven't got your wife behind you, you can't do many things."

Chavez spent most of the 1950s traveling to towns and settlements throughout the San Joaquin Valley. This photo shows migratory farm labor housing in the San Joaquin Valley in the 1950s.

The Chavezes had eight children, but Cesar's job required him to move every few months. Helen recalls one particularly difficult day when the family moved to El Rio, a small town near Oxnard, California, where her husband assumed leadership of a new Community Service Organization project:

> When we packed up in San Jose, we were so busy we forgot
> to go to the bank and get any money. The night before, Cesar
> had gotten sick and was just burning up with fever. I said,
> "let's wait." But we had everything packed, and he had a house
> meeting that evening. He said, "No; have to go."
>
> I don't drive, so he had to. Here we get into our beat-up
> station wagon loaded with this huge rented trailer with all
> our belongings in it and the kids, and I just had maybe a few
> dollars.
>
> We had to stop along the way because he was really burning
> up with fever, and I got a little something for the kids. Then
> the car stopped completely. We really didn't know what to do.
> Somebody stopped and helped us, so we gave them our last two
> dollars. The kids were hungry, but we didn't have any money to
> buy any food for them. Finally after that long trip, stopping all
> along the way, we got to El Rio. There was this little grocery

store, and I told Cesar "Go ask them if they'll cash a check for us because the kids haven't eaten since this morning." . . .

[Finally] we went up to the little house we had rented, but it was dark, and there was no electricity. I think we had a flashlight. We just threw a few mattresses on the floor so the kids could sleep. I fed them and put them to bed. Cesar went up to this meeting, sick as he was.

The Chavez family poses for a portrait in 1969. Six of their eight children are pictured.

■ TAKING ON THE BRACERO PROGRAM

In the summer of 1958, the CSO initiated a new project that required the Chavez family to move to Oxnard, a small coastal city in Ventura County north of Los Angeles. At the time, Oxnard was surrounded by lemon orchards and vegetable fields. The United Packinghouse Workers (UPW) union was having trouble organizing the laborers who packaged lemons for shipping nationwide. In an effort to help the Mexican American community and possibly convince workers to join the union, the UPW provided twenty thousand dollars to start a CSO chapter in Oxnard.

Chavez arrived expecting to register voters. But everyone he talked with complained about the braceros, the Mexicans imported by the federal government to work as cheap laborers for growers. Although Ventura County had a small population at the time, it had the largest community of braceros in the country. In Oxnard alone, the huge bracero camp housed more than twenty-eight thousand laborers. While Chavez and others felt compassion for the exploited Mexican workers, the Mexican American laborers were angry that the braceros were taking their jobs. As Chavez recalled:

> The jobs belonged to local workers. The braceros were brought only for exploitation. They were just instruments for the growers. Braceros didn't make any money, and they were exploited viciously, forced to work under conditions the local people wouldn't tolerate. If the braceros spoke up, if they made the minimal complaints, they'd be shipped back to Mexico. We . . . felt that ending the program would be the best thing we could do for them and for everybody.

Until this time, Chavez had been unfamiliar with the bracero program, but he quickly discovered that it was deeply corrupt. The program was based on a law that stated that workers could only be imported from Mexico during times of labor shortages. But agribusiness interests and labor department officials ignored this mandate and devised ways to get around the law.

In 1956, two years before Chavez took on the corrupt bracero program, Dr. Ernesto Galarza published a one-hundred-page pamphlet called *Strangers in Our Fields*. Galarza, who was research director for the National Agricultural Workers' Union, interviewed 350 Mexican bracero workers to document the abuses heaped upon them by growers. Several excerpts, in the workers' own words, appear below:

> I worked four weeks in the pea picking. The best pickers made three or four baskets a day. We were paying $1.75 a day for the board. I made so little I owed the camp restaurants $5.00 at the end of the month.

> We are installed in a barn occupied by the cows when we moved in. . . .

> Twenty men in one bunkhouse were sick to the stomach from rancid beans. . . . Some had to miss two or three days of work. They were charged for the meals for that time.

> You hear everywhere that they will send us back to Mexico if we are not content with the situation. . . .

> We noticed that the workers who complain get less work. They are transferred to the extra gang. This gang he says is for the loafers and the strikers.

The growers conspired with two government agencies that oversaw the bracero program, the Ventura County Farm Labor Association and the local office of the California Farm Placement Service. All migrant laborers, no matter where they were born, had to contract employment through these government offices. But the bureaucrats who ran the offices created barriers to prevent unemployed American farmworkers from applying for jobs. For example, whenever work was available, laborers were required to fill out official job applications that were so long and complicated, they took several hours to complete. By the time this frustrating task was over, braceros were already working in the fields.

■ ■ ■ ■ A BRIEF VICTORY IN VENTURA

Chavez began keeping meticulous records of every official job application and rejection. He studied the complex labor laws that governed the bracero program. Using this knowledge, he was able to notify state and federal investigators about the fraud that was taking place in Ventura County. This tactic took months of effort. But after Chavez filed more than one thousand separate complaints, federal labor investigators finally conducted a series of surprise inspections and ordered growers to hire local labor. This proved to be a temporary solution, however. Growers complied with the laws until the inspectors left the scene. Then the locals were fired and the braceros were put back to work.

With little in the way of success, Chavez was prompted to take direct action. In April 1959, hoping to awaken the public to the plight of Mexican American farmhands, Chavez organized a caravan of unemployed locals to march at dawn onto a tomato ranch where braceros were hard at work. The media had been notified, and reporters from newspapers, radio, and television arrived around the time the sheriff and highway patrol showed up to make arrests. When state labor officials arrived, they forced growers to hire Americans. The braceros were fired, and the local workers were hired to plant tomato seedlings for ninety cents an hour. But after police, inspectors, and the media left the scene, the locals were all fired. Braceros were back in the fields the next morning.

While the growers did not change their practices, the bureaucrats in charge of the program were investigated by the government. As a result, the chief of the California Farm Placement Service and two other top officials were forced to resign. Another bureau official, William Cunningham, was fired weeks before he was due to retire after it was shown he had taken bribes from growers to prevent local workers from obtaining employment.

Chavez moved to Los Angeles in late 1959, and the movement collapsed without his guidance. In Oxnard County, braceros continued to work in the fields while most locals remained unemployed. And the bruising fight took its toll on Chavez, who lost 25 pounds (11 kg) and grew ill from working twenty hours a day. However, the Ventura march was educational for him, and the tactics he used against the growers would prove useful in the future.

"A POT OF GOLD!"

Chavez felt that if he could have organized the local workers into a field-workers' union, they could have achieved a permanent victory. The CSO, however, would not allow it, because their focus was on helping the community. Their supporters did not want the organization to become involved in labor activity.

Although he remained angry and frustrated by the restrictions, Chavez agreed to take a job as executive director of the CSO. And by 1962, he had built the organization into twenty-two chapters in California and Arizona. The group helped countless Mexican Americans, registered tens of thousands of voters, and provided citizenship training to thousands more.

At the time, the CSO was the only large organization dedicated to helping Mexican Americans fight discrimination. As a result, it attracted dozens of strong leaders who would lead fights in the fields throughout the 1960s. One of those organizers was Dolores "Lola" Huerta, a mother of four small children who had a reputation as a fast-talking, outspoken, energetic, and aggressive leader. Huerta was born in 1930 in New Mexico, and she grew up in Stockton, California. She

Dolores Huerta *(left)* helps sign up workers in California for a labor organization in the early 1960s.

was raised by a single mother who was proud of her Mexican American heritage. She taught Dolores the ideal of *servicio*, a religious belief in generosity and modesty. As Huerta recalls, "You were not supposed to talk about what you did because if you did, then it removed the grace for that good deed." Although Huerta had two brothers, her independent mother broke with tradition and treated her daughter as an equal to her brothers. Unlike most Mexican families at the time, Huerta did not have to cook, sew, and clean for the men.

Like Chavez, Huerta was contacted by Fred Ross on the recommendation of a local priest. She joined the CSO in 1956, after Ross showed her some of the successful projects that the group had organized. Huerta was thrilled:

This was . . . something I had been looking for all my life. When Fred showed us pictures of people in Los Angeles that had come together, that had organized, that had fought the police and won, that had built health clinics, that had gotten people elected to office, I just felt like I had found a pot of gold! If organizing could make this happen, then this is definitely something I want to be part of.

Huerta was less excited when she met Chavez in 1958. Although she had been told repeatedly by Ross about his organizing prowess, the community leader did not make much of an impression. Huerta says he was very quiet and shy, and she did not even remember his face after their initial meeting. By 1962, however, Huerta and Chavez were close associates who had the same dream. They wanted to organize farm laborers into a union to fight for workers' rights and change the antiquated laws that favored agribusiness.

The priests who ran the CSO believed that a farmworkers' union could only be formed with the help of the American Federation of Labor/Congress of Industrial Organizations (AFL-CIO). At the time, this powerful union represented nearly all unionized workers in the United States. The AFL-CIO was not interested in helping farmworkers, however, so Chavez had to make one of the most difficult decisions of his life. He chose to quit the CSO and dedicate himself full-time to creating an independent farmworkers' union. This union would be able to force growers to sit down and bargain with those they had been exploiting for so long. The choice was not without risk, since Chavez would not be getting paid. But the family had about a thousand dollars in savings, and Chavez had the full support of Helen, who later recalled:

Cesar had always talked about organizing farm workers, even before the CSO. After all, we were both farm workers, and my parents and his parents and our whole families. Finally, he just made a decision that that's what he was going to do. He did discuss it and say it would be a lot of work and a lot of sacrifice because we wouldn't have any income coming in. But it didn't worry me. It didn't frighten me. . . . I never had any doubts that he would succeed. I thought a lot of people felt the way we did.

■ A MORE PERFECT UNION

Chavez announced he was quitting the CSO at the group's annual convention on March 31, 1962. Some members refused to accept his resignation and begged him to stay. Others wept openly. Chavez could not be deterred. In April he moved his family to Delano and rented the cheapest house he could find, setting up his office in the tiny, stifling hot garage. To support the family, Helen took a job picking grapes ten hours a day for eighty-five cents an hour.

Chavez decided to call his new group the National Farm Workers Association (NFWA). He envisioned the group as a culmination of his life's work, a crusade he called *el movimiento* (the movement). The following year, he explained the concept:

> The Farm Workers Association is a "movement" more than a "union" [because] once a movement begins it is impossible to stop. It will sweep through California and it will not be over until the farm worker has the equality of a living wage and decent treatment. . . . [A movement] is when the silent hopes of many people begin to become a real part of life.

Not only would the NFWA change the basic way migrant farmworkers lived, it would also be a place the poor could go for help. The organization would advocate for those who had wage disputes; late welfare checks; worker's compensation claims; and disputes with schools, hospitals, and the INS.

Chavez drew upon all the skills he had learned as a community organizer to jump-start the movement. He drew a map of the region and pinpointed eighty-six barrios and migrant worker camps to visit. He printed more than eighty thousand union registration cards for prospective members. With the aid of his children, whom he paid with ice cream, Chavez walked door-to-door in the barrios, handing out the cards and urging workers to join his new group.

Huerta, who was still working for the CSO, joined Chavez on weekends. Before long, however, Chavez convinced her to quit her job, move to Delano, and work full-time for the NFWA, saying "You can't work for a living and fight. You've got to do one or the other. You've got to do this full time." Chavez also called on family members to help build the association. He convinced his cousin Manuel Chavez, a car salesman in San Diego, to quit his job and help organize the group. And Chavez's brother, Richard, a carpenter, also made important contributions.

THE EAGLE FLIES

The NFWA held its first convention in September 1962, drawing 285 delegates to an abandoned theater in Fresno, California. Once the crowd was assembled, a dramatic scene occurred. The theater's movie screen was covered in paper, and on a signal from Chavez, the covering fell away to reveal a huge flag. It was the new symbol of the NFWA, designed by Richard Chavez. A black, square-edged eagle filled a white circle on a bloodred background. The eagle's head was taken from the Mexican flag, and the wings and body were meant to resemble an inverted Aztec temple, which symbolically linked the struggle to Mexican national identity.

The NFWA flag *(above)* became a strong and lasting symbol of the farmworker labor movement. In 1972, the UFWA became the United Farm Workers of America and joined the AFL-CIO as an independent member. This flag is from that period.

Dolores Huerta *(second from left)* **and Cesar Chavez** *(right)* **attend the founding convention of the National Farm Workers Association in 1962.**

There was an audible gasp from the crowd when the flag was revealed. Chavez hoped the symbol would inspire people, but some began walking out of the meeting. They thought the emblem looked like the flag of the Soviet Union or like the Nazi flag of the German Third Reich of the 1930s and 1940s. However, Manuel calmed the group by calling out, "When that damn eagle flies—that's when the farmworkers' problems are going to be solved!" After much debate, the flag was adopted as the official NFWA emblem along with the motto *Viva La Causa!* (Long Live the Cause!). Delegates also voted to charge members $3.50 a month so NFWA officials could receive a small salary.

After the excitement of the convention, a hard reality set in. Chavez and the others struggled to survive while working long days and driving countless miles across the Central Valley. Much of the food their families ate were donations from barrio residents. These residents shared what little they had with those who were working to improve

> "We didn't want a tractor or a crossed shovel and hoe or a guy with a hoe or pruning shears. . . . It was [my brother] Richard who suggested an eagle with square lines, an eagle anyone could make, with five steps in the wings."
>
> —Cesar Chavez, 1975

their lot. Although members paid union dues when they were working, most dropped out of the organization when unemployed. Meanwhile, Chavez refused a lucrative job paying twenty-one thousand dollars a year as director for the Peace Corps in Latin America. Dedicated to his principles, Chavez chose instead to build el movimiento from hard work, high principles, and a dream of equality.

CHAPTER 3

THE FIGHT
IS JOINED

The union was my *whole life*—I gave it more priority than my family. . . . I never thought of leaving the union, and I wanted to grow old working in the union on behalf of all farmworkers."

—Gilbert Padilla, codirector, National Farm Workers Association, 1980

In the summer of 1963, Cesar Chavez not only organized field hands, he also worked as one. His salary from the National Farm Workers Association was only fifty dollars a week. This was barely enough money to cover the gas and oil he burned in his 1959 Mercury station wagon driving hundreds of miles to attend house meetings. Consequently, Chavez chopped cotton, picked peas, and dug ditches to feed his eight children.

Chavez was not the only founding member of the NFWA who was making great personal sacrifices. Dolores Huerta, who had seven children, was going through a painful divorce. Her second husband, a former farmworker named Ventura Huerta, believed in la causa. But he also believed that his wife should spend more time at home taking care of their children. She had spent most of the past three years as a lobbyist for the CSO in Washington, D.C., and in Sacramento, the state capital. She spoke to senators and congressional representatives about labor laws and the ill treatment of migrant workers. In this era before women's liberation, Huerta played a unique role. She was the first woman to speak before a California senate committee. Her efforts helped legal immigrants gain retirement benefits for the first time.

SPEAKING MAN-TO-MAN

The political contacts Huerta made in the early 1960s proved invaluable when she went to work for the NFWA. As she joked to Chavez in a 1963 letter, "Being a now (ahem) experienced lobbyist, I am able to speak on a man-to-man basis with other lobbyists."

While male politicians were willing to listen to Huerta, tradition-bound field-workers found it more difficult to deal with a strong woman. There were times when she presided over NFWA meetings that some of the men refused to listen to her. Despite this treatment, in 1964 Huerta turned down a lucrative job with the state. She chose to remain with the NFWA, earning thirty dollars a week. To feed her seven children, she relied on government surplus food that union volunteers collected for her. Huerta, who had never worked in the fields, conceded that her early days with the NFWA were "a very, very hard time for us. But . . . this is what farmworker families go through every day of their lives."

■ ■ ■ ■ THE FIRST STRIKE

One of Huerta's associates at the NFWA, Gilbert Padilla, was intimately familiar with the hardships of being a farmworker. Padilla was born in a migrant camp in 1925 and was raised in the fields. As a child, he worked picking lettuce, beans, cotton, tomatoes, and other crops with his mother, father, brothers, and sister. His experiences in the fields inspired him to resist injustice, and he became one of Chavez's closest advisers after joining the CSO in 1955.

In addition to working with the CSO, Padilla was a member of the California Migrant Ministry (CMM). This group was founded in the 1950s to establish Christian ministries on the outskirts of small farm towns where migrant laborers settled. Unlike leaders of mainstream churches, who generally supported large growers, the CMM strived to promote justice and independence among farmworkers. During the late 1950s, members of the ministry received training from Fred Ross and Chavez and the CMM was closely associated with the farmworkers' struggles.

In the summer of 1965, Padilla and CMM member Jim Drake took on California bureaucrats over the squalid housing in the state-owned labor camps in Tulare County. Tulare County, in the fertile San Joaquin Valley, has long been one of the leading producers of agricultural

Gilbert Padilla *(center)* speaks at a farmworkers' strike meeting in the 1960s.

commodities in the United States. During the Depression, jobs available at ranches, food processing plants, and shipping warehouses attracted thousands of workers. The agribusiness interests were unprepared for this flood of itinerate laborers. They used their political power to convince the state to provide temporary housing for the workers. The state hastily erected dozens of flimsy tin shacks with no running water.

Thirty years later, the Depression-era shacks had become a permanent part of the landscape in the towns of Woodville and Linnell. They were managed by a state bureaucracy called the Tulare County Housing Authority (TCHA). The TCHA was making a good profit renting the substandard shacks to migrant families for about twenty-two dollars a month. The housing authority wanted to double the rent, despite that the shacks had been condemned by the county health department. When Padilla and Drake heard about this, they organized protest marches and a rent strike. The NFWA joined in the rent strike, and for the first time, the red, black, and white eagle flag flew over a labor camp.

A child stands in front of a typical home in a farm labor camp. The shacks lacked electricity and running water.

During the rent strike, renters stopped paying the TCHA. Instead, the six hundred people who lived in the two camps placed their money into a trust fund. Finally, after two years, the strike was successfully resolved in favor of the workers. Improvements were made to the living quarters, and the rents were not raised.

■ LET FREEDOM RING

The Tulare rent strike took place at a time when Americans were joining progressive political groups in unprecedented numbers. The civil rights movement, led by Dr. Martin Luther King Jr., had captured the public's imagination. Millions of idealistic young people of all races were entering college. They were eager to participate in protest marches, voter registration drives, and civil rights rallies. Many of these activities were organized by student groups such as the Student Nonviolent Coordinating Committee (SNCC).

On the West Coast, the growing social movement was centered in Berkeley at the University of California. While the nation was largely focused on African American rights, many in California were heartened by a line in King's famous "I have a dream" speech, delivered on August 28, 1963: "Let freedom ring from the curvaceous peaks of California." Thousands of students took this to mean that they should head into the fields to fight

Martin Luther King Jr. delivers his "I have a dream" speech in Washington, D.C., on August 28, 1963.

for Mexican American rights. Doug Adair, a graduate student in history who loved to garden, was one of those people. During the summer of 1965, he decided to travel to the San Joaquin Valley to pick plums and peaches and learn about agribusiness firsthand.

Having grown up in the upper-middle-class town of Claremont in Southern California, Adair was appalled by what he found. After he was hired, he was taken to his living quarters, a run-down shack in the TCHA labor camp. He discovered the tiny tin huts had no window glass or screens and were hot as ovens in the summer sun. Some shacks housed families with eight members. Adair also found there were no bathrooms in the fields, and growers charged workers five cents for a cup of ice water and up to fifty cents for a soda that cost a dime at the grocery store.

Adair also confronted a more serious problem. The labor contractor was deducting Social Security from workers' paychecks and keeping the money instead of sending it to the government as required by federal law. When Adair looked into the situation, which had been going on for years, he discovered no local officials could stop the practice. Instead, it was up to each worker to confront the contractor. Few did. The workers knew they would be labeled as troublemakers and blacklisted.

■ THE VOICE OF THE FARM WORKER

Because he was not dependent on the growers, Adair became a spokesperson for the angry workers. During the rent strike, he befriended Padilla, who took him to Delano to meet Chavez and Huerta. Adair had a shiny new pickup truck, so Chavez asked him if he could use it to deliver the NFWA newspaper, El Malcriado: The Voice of the Farm Worker. Adair readily agreed and was soon an integral part of the worker organization. Instead of returning to Berkeley that fall to finish his courses, Adair took a job writing for the English-language edition of El Malcriado.

Huerta and Chavez started El Malcriado in 1964. The name means "ill-bred" or "children who speak back to their parents." This was understood as a sly joke among Spanish-speaking readers, who believed that growers often dismissed worker demands as if they were coming from naughty children. Despite the humorous title, El Malcriado printed scathing political cartoons and articles that used satire, ridicule, and irony to criticize growers for low wages, poor working conditions, and the use of dangerous pesticides.

The cartoons by farmworker and artist Andy Zermeno were among the most popular features in El Malcriado. Since many migrant workers could not read, Zermeno created three characters who were instantly recognizable to field hands. Patroncito was the overweight grower with dark sunglasses, a cowboy hat, and a giant belt buckle over his swollen belly. Zermeno says Patroncito "can be seen almost anywhere you go in California, speeding along in his Cadillac or counting money in an office, or once in a while walking between the rows, worrying about his grapes, or talking to his field boss. The only time he ever talks to [a field-worker] is when he needs him. And when he no longer needs him he throws him away."

The field boss is named Coyote. He is a mean man who does Patroncito's bidding. The hapless field-worker is Don Sotaco. Sotaco must struggle against Coyote and Patroncito. Although he is often afraid, Sotaco understands he must overcome his fear because "the fight is not going to end until Patroncito has been cut down to size."

These characters helped create a great demand for El Malcriado. Ten-cent copies of the biweekly paper sold out at barrio grocery stores nearly as fast as Chavez could deliver them. When Chavez began printing an English version, the number of subscriptions increased rapidly.

Students and farmworkers were not the only ones interested in El Malcriado. Growers could also buy the paper, and many felt threatened by the articles that exposed their corrupt practices to a large audience. Some growers complained to the FBI, and agents began poring over the pages of the paper. Although El Malcriado was advocating equal rights for workers and exposing illegal acts by growers, the FBI considered Chavez a possible threat to national security. The bureau opened a file called "COMINFIL: Communist Infiltration of the National Farm Workers Association." During the decade that followed, Chavez's FBI file would grow to more than two thousand pages.

These men are performing a play with the characters from
El Malcriado. The characters became a fixture in public relations and
recruiting for the farmworkers.

■ ■ ■ ■ "ONLY THE BEGINNING"

Perhaps authorities were right to fear the articles in El Malcriado. For the first time, rootless migrant workers had a centralized voice. The paper not only spread the message about the NFWA but also acted as a forum for workers to publicize their grievances. If a contractor pocketed Social Security funds or overcharged laborers for rancid beans, it was no longer an isolated incident. The victims could notify El Malcriado, and the newspaper would expose the criminal acts to readers from the vineyards of Delano to the college campuses of the San Francisco Bay Area. Bolstered by the unifying voice of the paper, workers were starting to feel their power.

One labor dispute thoroughly covered by El Malcriado concerned the controversial bracero program in the Coachella Valley, about 150 miles (241 kilometers) east of Los Angeles. The bracero program was officially ended by an act of Congress in 1964. But growers bitterly complained to California governor Pat Brown that there would be severe labor shortages because of the termination of the program. Brown lobbied President Lyndon B. Johnson to allow braceros back into the country. The president relented, as long as the laborers were paid $1.40 an hour, 15¢ more than the minimum wage at that time.

The Coachella Valley is an extremely hot desert region where grapes are grown in the winter and harvested in spring. In March 1965, when Filipino American workers arrived to work in the vineyards, they were told they would be paid the minimum wage, $1.25 an hour. When they discovered that the braceros were earning $1.40 an hour, the Agricultural Workers Organizing Committee called a strike.

AWOC was organized by Filipino farmworker Larry D. Itliong. The group had been fighting for job security, union recognition, and better working conditions for its members since 1959. Since most Filipino workers belonged to AWOC, the Coachella strike achieved success within ten days, and the workers were all paid $1.40 an hour. As the harvest moved north throughout the summer, AWOC pressured growers to pay the higher wage.

The AWOC victories were closely covered in El Malcriado. In one article, Chavez wrote, "We who are picking the grapes and the peaches and tomatoes, which are the lifeblood of California, are soon going to share in the richness we have made. The little fights against the little grower and contracts that you read about today are only the beginning."

■ "WE NEEDED MONEY"

AWOC was emboldened by its success at achieving higher wages for its members. But when the grape harvest began in Delano in early September, workers were informed by the nine vineyards in the region that they would only be paid $1 an hour. Since this was the last big harvest before winter, most found this unacceptable. Jobs would be difficult to find in the coming months, and workers needed money to get them through the off-season. Itliong sent letters to the growers demanding $1.40 an hour for his union members, but no growers replied.

As "strike fever" spread among workers, Itliong visited Chavez. He asked him if the NFWA was a union or a civil rights organization. Chavez said it was a union but had no plans to call a strike. At the time, the NFWA had twelve hundred members, but only about two hundred were paying dues. Chavez did not think the organization would be powerful enough to call a strike for at least three years. But on the evening of September 7, a group of Filipino workers sat down in the fields at Lucas and Sons vineyards and refused to move, bringing work to a stop. The next morning, Filipinos in nine labor camps went on strike under the AWOC banner. By the end of the day, eleven more labor camps had joined the strike. It was the largest strike in the Delano vineyards since the 1930s.

Chavez learned about the strike on the morning of September 8. He quickly called a meeting of NFWA board members. They unanimously agreed to join the strike. Chavez understood the task ahead would be long and arduous, but as he later wrote, he had a plan for victory:

> I knew that the only way we could win was to keep fighting for a long time . . . and that the only way we could win was by staying with it. . . . We talked about the need to make the strike a

public controversy as soon as possible to get it out of the Delano area, not letting the growers choke it there, but publicizing it. I was sure we couldn't win by ourselves. We needed money. And in order for the growers to come out with what they really thought of the Unions, the best way was to put them under pressure and let them express themselves in public.

What the NFWA lacked in funds, it made up for in organizational skills and dedicated members. Itliong and Chavez both understood that if the Mexican American community did not support the strike, it would fail because Mexican American workers would be hired to replace the Filipinos. Traditionally, growers pitted Mexican Americans and Filipinos against one another to maintain power over the divided groups. Therefore, it was up to the NFWA to convince its members to join what quickly became known in Spanish as *La Huelga* (the Strike).

Chavez called an emergency meeting of the NFWA on September 16 so members could vote on whether or not to join the strikers. The choice of the date was no accident. It was Mexican Independence Day, the holiday that marked the end of Spanish rule over Mexico in 1810. To draw support for the effort, Chavez inserted a leaflet in *El Malcriado* that read: "Now is when every worker, without regard to race, color, and nationality, should support the strike and under no circumstances work in those ranches that have been struck."

■ THE FIRST DAYS

While Chavez worked to organize the NFWA, the grape strike continued to grow. By the second day, more than two thousand Filipino farmhands were on strike. The men still lived at labor camps owned by those who were being struck. Eugene Nelson, who worked as a picket line organizer during the first days of the strike, described the retaliation by the growers:

> We hear . . . of men being evicted from their [labor] camps, men who had lived and worked there for twenty years, evicted

because they asked for a twenty-cent-an-hour raise. At one camp the men are locked out just before dinner; they are forced to cook alongside the road. A cop comes along and kicks their cooking pot over. Suitcases and other gear are dumped out on the road; workers are afraid to return for their cars for fear of being arrested for trespassing. At other camps all the utilities are shut off, but the determined strikers stay in the camps; if they leave they will have no place to go. . . . They decide to stick it out in the face of the threats of armed security guards, one of whom has already shot at a striker who did not move fast enough.

By the fifth day of the strike, with a ripe crop of grapes hanging on the vines, the growers took another measure to bring in the harvest. Two buses of strikebreakers, known as scabs, were brought from Fresno and Los Angeles.

In addition to employing scab labor, the growers pursued various legal means to end the strike. They obtained court orders called injunctions that sharply limited the number of strikers who could picket in a particular place. Injunctions were also issued to limit noise, so police could arrest strikers who were singing, chanting, or cursing at the scabs. However, most arrested under these orders were immediately released since the injunctions violated the Constitution's protections concerning free speech and the right to free assembly.

"VIVA LA HUELGA!"

By the September 16 NFWA meeting, strike fever had infected nearly everyone in the area. More than fifteen hundred people packed into Our Lady of Guadalupe Church, which Chavez had rented for the meeting. The NFWA flag adorned the wall behind the stage along with a large picture of Emiliano Zapata, a Mexican revolutionary of the early 1900s. A third poster contained the words of a short essay called "Definition of a Strikebreaker," written in 1903 by legendary California author Jack

Strikers try to convince a scab to join the Delano grape strike in 1966.

London, which began, "After God had finished the rattlesnake, the toad, and the vampire, he had some awful substance left with which he made a scab."

London's words and the general mood of the rowdy crowd frightened police, growers, and others in Delano. However, when Chavez took the stage, he urged the crowd to remain peaceful: "We are engaged in . . . [a] struggle for the freedom and dignity which poverty denies us. But it must not be a violent struggle, even if violence is used against us. Violence can only hurt our cause."

After Chavez spoke, workers rose to describe the hardships they had suffered in the past. Most felt it was their honor and duty to support their Filipino colleagues by going out on strike. The crowd began to chant "Viva la huelga! Viva la causa!" (Long live the strike! Long live the cause!). When it was announced that the vote supported joining the strike, the crowd erupted in a ten-minute roar that shook the rafters of the old church.

With the Mexican Americans and Filipinos together, work would cease on forty-eight vineyards. The enthusiasm helped swell the ranks of the NFWA. Twenty-seven hundred new members joined the union after the meeting.

■ VIOLENCE AND NONVIOLENCE

The days after the meeting were hectic at the small NFWA office set up in a corner store on First and Albany streets in Delano. Union members were using the cramped space, no bigger than 20 by 40 feet (6 by 12 m), as an office, service center, dormitory, and meeting hall. In addition, reporters, TV camera operators, ministers, politicians, and volunteers from the cities came and went. Hundreds of "Huelga" picket signs were painted. Picket crews were formed, each with a captain who would organize the strike team and maintain peace on the picket lines. Meanwhile, deputies, highway patrol officers, FBI agents, and sheriffs maintained a constant presence. Nelson recalls that they were "following us everywhere, taking thousands of pictures, with movie and still cameras both, seemingly trying to get something on us . . . and they succeed in scaring off some of the more recent arrivals from Mexico who do not know their supposed rights."

On September 19, Chavez held a meeting with Al Green, leader of AWOC. The two signed a historic agreement that the NFWA and AWOC would work together to achieve an increase in wages for the grape workers to $1.40 an hour plus 25¢ for each filled box. A joint strike committee was set up, and the two union leaders were photographed together. Green also agreed to feed the strikers at AWOC headquarters in the Filipino Hall for as long as the strike lasted. For the cash-strapped NFWA members, this was very good news. As Chavez recalled, on a financial level, the NFWA "had nothing to give . . . except our love . . . while the Filipinos had money and they had a hall and food which they . . . shared with us, not only because of Union solidarity but because of the Filipino culture. They're beautiful about helping people."

Life on the picket lines, however, was less than beautiful. Picketers gathered around vineyard entrances with signs in Spanish, English, and Tagalog, all accompanied by the NFWA black eagle. Police and big-city private detectives hired by growers kept a close watch on the picketers, ready to arrest protesters for trespassing if they stepped onto ranch property.

Growers used many tactics to intimidate and harass the picketers. Assured that the strikers would maintain a position of nonviolence, growers were free to push protesters, punch them, and jab elbows into their ribs. Most growers carried loaded shotguns and wore pistols. They used vicious barking dogs to lunge at strikers. In one

An armed grower guards his fields during the grape strike in Delano in 1966.

Issue no. 22 of El *Malcriado* provided a list of contributions from those providing aid to the strikers:

In Santa Rosa, school children each brought two cans of food in a paper bag for the strikers. The Association got about 100 little bags of canned food for the strike store.

In Corcoran . . . a member of the Association was working in another crop. At the end of last week, he came to the office and presented Cesar Chavez with his whole paycheck as a contribution for the strike.

Students from [the University of California] Berkeley set up tables all over town and talked to everybody on the streets about the strike. Last weekend they came to Delano with a large truckload of food and a contribution of money. Sacramento students . . . collected so much food that it was necessary to rent a 5-ton [4.5-metric-ton] truck to bring it to Delano.

instance, a grower chased off picketers with a shotgun and set their picket signs on fire. When they did not burn fast enough for him, he blasted the signs with his shotgun. Another grower fired his gun over the heads of picketers. Growers also used machinery as a weapon. It was common for ranchers and managers to drive their cars directly at the picket lines at a high speed, swerving away at the last minute. Others drove tractors up and down dirt roads, raising choking clouds of dust.

In several cases, pesticide spraying equipment was used to drench picketers with deadly sulfur, which temporarily blinded them. The most severe incident of this type was perpetrated by Jack Radovich Jr., who carried out a sulfur attack, blinding sixteen people. Police refused to prosecute the eighteen-year-old son of a wealthy rancher. According to El Malcriado, "The sheriff explained that the procedure for obtaining the arrest . . . of Radovich was very difficult and involved the highway patrol, the district attorney, trips to Bakersfield, and long distance phone calls at our expense."

Although many picketers wanted to strike back against those who harmed them, Chavez continued to preach nonviolence:

> If someone commits violence against us, it is much better—if we can—not to react against the violence, but to react in such a way as to get closer to our goal. People don't like to see a nonviolent movement subjected to violence, and there's a lot of support across the country for nonviolence. That's the key point we have going for us. We can turn the world if we can do it nonviolently."

"PLAIN **HOODLUMS!**"

The Delano grape strikers maintained a nonviolent stance. This allowed growers, foremen, and strikebreakers to insult and physically attack them while police did nothing. In one instance, strikers were protesting in front of a scab's house when eight drunken growers began throwing punches and stomping on toes. Picketers did not react, and police looked the other way. Eugene Nelson, who grew up on a local ranch, was appalled after witnessing this behavior. He stated that the growers acted like hoodlums in a New York street gang.

A grower uses a tractor to create clouds of dust near strikers during the Delano grape strike.

■ MOTHERS AGAINST CHAVEZ

By October 1965, Chavez, Huerta, and Padilla were rising before dawn each morning. They spent their days organizing strikers and picket lines to cover the 450-square-mile (1,166 sq. km) area of Kern and Tulare counties. The work was difficult, but the strike was attracting media attention. Newspapers were referring to events in the Central Valley as "The Great Delano Grape Strike." Still, Chavez feared the action might turn into an unsuccessful standoff between growers and strikers.

To make the strike a statewide issue, Chavez began traveling to churches and campuses, where he spoke about the plight of the farmworkers. After explaining the issues to mostly white, middle-class audiences, he asked for donations of money, food, and clothing, which were desperately needed with winter approaching. But Chavez wanted more from his listeners, and he implored people to visit Delano and help with the strike or at least observe the daily harassment directed at picketers.

Chavez's tactic worked. Outsiders streamed into the area. This created tension among the citizens of Delano, who were dependent on growers for their business. They were not accustomed to strangers observing them and referred to the newcomers as outside agitators, subversives, Communists, and peaceniks. Growers felt it was their right to treat workers as they had for generations, and they formed committees to put forth their arguments. Groups such as Mothers Against Chavez and Citizens for Facts organized counter-picket lines, with signs that urged outsiders to go home.

As autumn turned to winter, the hopes of the Delano grape strikers fell with the temperatures. Few were willing to stand in the cold and

Not all picketers supported the NFWA. This picket sign from the mid-1960s was probably carried by a grape grower or a supporter of the growers.

> "FACTS ARE: Chavez and his cohorts have imported the long-haired kooks, professional loafers, winos, and dregs of society to carry the Huelga [strike] banners. The true farm workers are in the fields working."
>
> —Citizens for *Facts* leaflet, 1965

picket empty fields. Most of the scabs had gone back to Mexico or moved on to harvest vegetables in the desert. But Chavez was undeterred. In a little office in the small town of Delano, Chavez, Padilla, and Huerta drew up plans to draw national attention to the protest. The 1965 harvest was finished, but Chavez felt la causa was just beginning.

CHAPTER 4

NATIONAL
BOYCOTTS

"We are suffering. We have suffered. . . . Now we will suffer for the purpose of ending the poverty, the misery, and the injustice, with the hope that our children will not be exploited as we have been."

—National Farm Workers Association, "Proclamation 1966," 1966

During his years of organizing, Cesar Chavez had seen many strikes achieve short-term victories only to fail in the long run. In his experience, growers were able to retain their political power, while workers had only a temporary advantage when fruit was ripe in the fields. To change this situation, the NFWA would have to encourage politicians in Sacramento and Washington, D.C., to make permanent changes in labor laws. But to gain political support, it would be necessary to educate American voters about the plight of farmworkers. To do this, the Delano grape strike would have to become a national issue that would generate headlines in big-city newspapers. This meant taking on Schenley Industries, a multinational liquor company, which was the biggest grape grower in the region.

Schenley was world famous for its best-selling brands such as Cutty Sark whiskey. The company also sold a variety of liqueurs, brandies, and Roma wine, all made from grapes produced on a 4,500-acre (1,821-hectare) vineyard near Delano. Although the company earned $250 million in annual sales, the labor camp at Schenley's vineyard had changed little since the 1910s. Workers lived in unheated tin shacks without window screens, running water, or indoor kitchen facilities. And like other growers in the region, Schenley refused to meet the $1.40-an-hour wage demand by the strikers.

BOYCOTTS AND PICKETERS

In February 1966, Chavez gathered a group of strikers, organizers, and supporters for a three-day meeting to figure out how to go after Schenley. It was agreed that the NFWA and AWOC would institute a consumer boycott to convince the public not to buy Schenley products. A boycott was seen as a good strategy because, unlike grapes, the company's brands were easily identified by the public. The boycott would not only hurt the company's profits but could generate stories in the media. This would embarrass the company and tarnish its image as a producer of high-quality products.

To enact the boycott, the NFWA began picketing the company's San Francisco office. The union also sent letters to liquor stores and supermarkets in Los Angeles, San Francisco, and elsewhere, asking managers to remove Schenley products from their shelves. They were also asked to place a poster supporting the grape strike in their windows. Those who refused were subject to picketing by small teams of two to three protesters. The teams handed out leaflets about Schenley labor practices. Ever aware of maintaining a peaceful image, Chavez warned workers not to block store entrances or speak with truck drivers unloading Schenley products. In detailed instructions, Chavez wrote:

> Do not argue with, harass, or intimidate anyone, whether it is a consumer, a store manager or an employee. Do not force a handbill on anyone and if they are thrown away by consumers, pick them up promptly.... The National Farm Workers Association may be held answerable for your conduct, so you are not to drink or fight or carry weapons of any sort, or swear, or engage in any conduct which might be classified as boisterous.

To broaden the scope of the boycott, several NFWA members hitchhiked from California to New York City to work with the Student Nonviolent Coordinating Committee. The SNCC and NFWA organized a letter-writing campaign to encourage consumers to send hundreds of letters to Schenley to voice their support for the Delano grape workers. The activists also sent letters to New York City liquor stores asking them to remove Schenley products or face picketers.

PILGRIMAGE, PENITENCE, AND REVOLUTION

Positioning pickets at liquor stores and markets was only one part of the NFWA strategy. The group also raised the idea of holding a massive farmworkers' march from Delano to Sacramento. At a distance of 250 miles (402 km), this would be the longest protest march in U.S. history. Such an event would make a major media impact and draw national attention to the boycott.

The long walk was planned to begin in mid-March 1966 with protesters arriving in Sacramento on April 10, Easter Sunday. Planners felt that linking Easter Sunday to the farmworkers' struggle was appropriate. Almost all the strikers were Catholic, and during demonstrations, union members often carried crosses and portraits of the Virgin of Guadalupe, the Mexican depiction of the Virgin Mary.

THE VIRGIN OF GUADALUPE

Whenever the NFWA organized rallies or protest marches, strikers displayed images of the Virgin of Guadalupe (*below*). As the Mexican representation of the Virgin Mary, the Virgin of Guadalupe held enormous religious, political, and social meaning for Chavez and his followers. She represented not only the Catholic Church but also the spiritual mother who provided protection and liberation from oppressors. The Virgin of Guadalupe was always there to help the poor. Her image gave strength to the strikers, who believed they would triumph in their struggle if their faith was strong.

The religious imagery also appealed to mainstream Americans, while simultaneously silencing critics who tried to link the farmworkers to what was called godless Communism. (The Soviet Union was an atheist state.)

Chavez wanted the long walk to Sacramento to promote this strong religious message, so he chose the theme "Pilgrimage, Penitence, and Revolution" for the march. He understood that the

EL TEATRO CAMPESINO

El Teatro Campesino got its start performing short plays for laborers in the fields of California's Central Valley in 1965. The theater company was founded by Delano native Luis Valdez, one of ten children in a family of farmworkers. Valdez was the first member of his family to attend college, where he studied theater and drama. After graduation he returned to Delano to help Cesar Chavez with the grape strike. Since

Chavez *(left)* stands in New York with El Teatro Campesino founder Luis Valdez in the 1970s. They are standing in front of an advertisement for *Zoot Suit*, a play written and directed for Broadway by Valdez.

practice of pilgrimage is something deeply rooted in Mexican culture. Millions of people make pilgrimages to the Basilica of Our Lady of Guadalupe in Mexico City. Sometimes they crawl to the church on their hands and knees, praying for assistance from saints and the Virgin of Guadalupe. Chavez believed that many farmworkers would be persuaded to join the march because they saw themselves engaged in pilgrimages.

many farmworkers were illiterate, Valdez created El Teatro Campesino to teach social, political, and economic lessons through humorous and dramatic skits.

The actors in the Teatro were farmworkers who often drew on their experiences for material. Performances took place on the backs of flatbed trucks with no scenery and no costumes. Actors hung signs around their necks to indicate the characters they were playing. In the early years, the Teatro taught audiences about the grape strike, worker rights, civil rights, and Mexican American history. During the late 1960s, the Teatro expanded its subject matter to cover education, the Vietnam War, indigenous roots, and racism. Between 1965 and 1967, El Teatro Campesino went on a national tour to raise funds for the striking farmworkers. From 1969 through 1980, the Teatro toured across the United States and Mexico and made six tours to Europe.

The NFWA also wanted to link the concepts of religious pilgrimages with the American tradition of secular (nonreligious) protest. This was done through the theater group El Teatro Campesino (the Farmworkers Theater). El Teatro used one-act plays to teach illiterate workers about protest, civil rights, and activism.

The second aspect of the theme, penitence, was meant to remind Mexican Americans of religious sacrifice and God's forgiveness of sins. The march was taking place during the Lenten season. On the final day of Lent, people in some Mexican communities reenact the final days of Jesus from his Last Supper to his Crucifixion. Chavez tied this to the long walk to Sacramento, during which the marchers would likely suffer from hunger, thirst, heat, and fatigue.

Not everyone involved with the movement supported the religious symbolism promoted by Chavez. Antonio Orendain, who had been secretary-treasurer of the NFWA since its inception, did not believe in mixing religion and union activities. Another prominent union member, Epifanio Camacho, was a Communist who did not believe in God. In reference to the Virgin of Guadalupe, he pasted a bumper sticker on his truck that read "I Too Was a Virgin Once," which created controversy among the more religious protesters.

Chavez ignored the doubters because Gandhi and Martin Luther King Jr. both considered spiritual penance and purification essential for nonviolent resistance. But it was the third element that was considered most controversial. Chavez considered the march a revolutionary act. He believed that the term represented Mexican revolutionaries who fought against large landowners in the 1920s. As he wrote in the "Plan for Delano":

> We shall pursue the REVOLUTION we have proposed. We are sons of the Mexican Revolution, a revolution seeking bread and justice. Our revolution will not be armed, but we want the existing social order to dissolve. . . . We are poor, we are humble, and our only choice is to strike in those ranches where we are not treated with the respect we deserve as working men, where our rights as free and sovereign men are not recognized.

To those who oppose us, be they ranchers, police, politicians, or speculators, we say that we are going to continue fighting until we die, or we win. WE SHALL OVERCOME.

■ ■ ■ KENNEDY WALKS THE PICKET LINE

On March 14, 1966, three days before the long walk was to begin, another revolutionary event took place. For the first time in history, a U.S. Senate subcommittee traveled to Delano to investigate living and working conditions of farm laborers. One of the members of the Subcommittee on Migratory Labor was Robert Kennedy, a Democratic U.S. senator from New York and brother of former president John F. Kennedy, who had been assassinated in November 1963.

Chavez testified before the committee and presented hard evidence of police bias against the strikers. He also showed that growers

Chavez *(center)* testifies during U.S. Senate subcommittee meetings in California on March 14, 1966.

had illegally imported Mexican workers as strikebreakers. Chavez reminded the senators that every laborer in the United States, except the farmworker, was protected by child labor laws, was guaranteed a minimum wage, and was provided the right to organize unions. Farmworkers had no such protections because of a "farm lobby . . . in the thirties which forced [the government] to decide that farmwork and farmworkers were somehow different from everyone else."

Chavez was not the only speaker to make an impression on the senators. On March 16, Kern County sheriff Roy Galyen testified that he had ordered deputies to photograph picketers and interview them so the department could compile dossiers, or legal files, on the individuals. The sheriff also said he had arrested protesters when he heard rumors that there might be riots on the picket lines. These actions disturbed Kennedy because the strikers had committed no crimes. The room erupted with derisive laughter when Kennedy suggested that the sheriff spend some time reading the Constitution of the United States to prevent further violation of farmworkers' rights. Later that day, Kennedy became the first senator ever to march on a picket line. He joined Chavez and other strikers at the DiGiorgio Fruit Corporation's 4,400-acre (1,780-hectare) ranch.

DiGiorgio was a powerful company that farmed more than 18,000 acres (7,284 hectares) of grapes, plums, apricots, pears, and vegetables on ranches from Delano to Borrego Springs outside San Diego. These fruits were sold fresh or canned in grocery stores coast-to-coast. The fact that a U.S. senator was joining a protest against this powerful corporation created incredible excitement. Paul Schrade, an official with the United Automobile Workers (UAW) union, who was picketing DiGiorgio that day recalls:

> One of the best moments I have had in my whole life was marching in front of the DiGiorgio Ranch where there was this half-mile [0.8 km] picket line of farmworkers under the blue skies and in the wide open spaces of the San Joaquin Valley and Bob [Kennedy] came marching down the line shaking hands with all of the pickets. And you could hear coming

Senator Robert Kennedy *(right)* visits with Chavez on the picket line in 1966.

from a distance these great voices shouting 'Viva Kennedy' and 'Kennedy por presidente' [for president] and it was a great time when you knew that friendship had been cemented and Bob wouldn't forget; that the farmworkers wouldn't forget. It really was very important towards building the movement.

In the months that followed, Kennedy honored the boycott, refusing to buy Schenley products. Kennedy's wife, Ethel, raised money for the boycott, holding fund-raisers with wealthy celebrities and politicians. Kennedy also became a close friend of Chavez and offered important strategic advice to movement leaders. The senator's help proved to be invaluable to the farmworkers' movement. As Kennedy aide Peter Edelman later wrote, "Kennedy's concern for the farm workers ... plugged Chavez into the power outlets in Washington and New York. For the first time, Chavez became fashionable, a national figure."

■ PEACEABLE WORK

It is doubtful that Chavez felt like a powerful national figure when he led the march out of Delano the morning after Kennedy walked the picket line. About one hundred ragtag protesters headed down Highway 99, slowly snaking northward to Ducor, the first planned stop, 21 miles (34 km) away.

Some of the marchers were not farmworkers but FBI agents who had infiltrated the NFWA. The FBI knew the exact route the marchers would take and shared the information with U.S. Army commanders in Pasadena. The army put troops on alert in case riots broke out.

The FBI later reported that the protesters were about 75 percent Mexican Americans or Filipinos. In addition to one or two African Americans, the rest were white. And just as Chavez had planned, the national press corps was also in attendance. The next day, newspapers carried dramatic photos of farmworkers marching in the hot sun. They were holding many cloth banners with images of the Virgin of Guadalupe and the NFWA black eagle. They also held flags of AWOC, Mexico, the United States, and the Philippines. Some even shouldered large crosses to represent the final journey of Jesus. Veterans of World War II (1939–1945) and the Korean War (1950–1953) proudly displayed medals awarded to them by the armed forces.

The size of the crowd swelled when the marchers reached each new settlement. As they approached Porterville on the second day, the group was met at the edge of town by several hundred supporters, some with guitars and accordions. The voices of the protesters rose in song as they made their way through the small village. As the sun fell, the group set up camp in a local park. Shoes and socks were stripped off aching feet, and Peggy McGivern, the NFWA nurse, treated blisters.

The activities did not end at dark. The encampment attracted hundreds of townspeople. The union planned for this and had educational programs featuring singing, speeches, and skits by El Teatro Campesino. People were also asked to sign a pledge supporting the boycott and mail it to Schenley. The pledge demanded: "Get with it Schenley, and negotiate. Recognize the National Farm Workers Association!"

The scene in Porterville was reenacted every night as the protesters marched through small towns and large cities such as Fresno. In Parlier, supporters cooked a huge dinner feast for the marchers and served it at the Catholic church in the barrio. In other towns, dinners were held in community halls. To ensure the protesters received breakfast, volunteers spread out at night asking locals to cook in the morning. Those who signed up were educated about union efforts as they served beans, eggs, and coffee.

While the march had festive elements, the pain of walking more than 10 to 15 miles (16 to 24 km) per day was nearly unbearable for some. Chavez suffered from a swollen ankle and severe blisters. For the first week of the march, he was running a high fever caused by his injuries. It was not until the fifteenth day of the march that he could walk without searing pain. Others had blood seeping out of their shoes as they limped along. While these ailments caused some to drop out,

Chavez *(center with cane)* and other marchers continue toward Sacramento on March 21, 1966, despite physical pain.

several dozen people walked every step of the way. Chavez explains the feelings that kept them going:

> There's something about a march that is very powerful. It's a powerful weapon, a powerful organizing tool, and it has a powerful influence on those who participate. There is this anticipation. You have a definite starting place and a definite goal. You're moving, making progress every step. That's very comforting to people. It gives a great sense of calm, because it's peaceable work. . . . Then there's the personal sense of sacrifice.

■ SCHENLEY SIGNS WITH THE UNION

By the third week of the long walk, the protest had been covered nationally by newspapers, magazines, and news shows. Enthusiastic crowds greeted the marchers in nearly every town. When the strikers walked into Stockton, more than five thousand were there to cheer them on. People threw flowers and offered food and money while mariachi musicians took the lead, playing joyous music. The protest turned into a fiesta, and it took the marchers more than two hours to walk 3 miles (5 km) through town.

Grape strikers march through Stockton, California, in March 1966

Cesar Chavez discusses the pain he suffered while marching the 250 miles (402 km) from Delano to Sacramento:

> I had a rough and miserable time at the beginning. Before we started everybody was getting their feet ready for the march. But I was so busy I didn't have time to get ready. I was very tired and out of shape. While others had gotten boots, all I had were some old worn-out low shoes. My back already was bothering me when we started, so I began to favor one foot, which caused blisters on the other. By the time we got to Richgrove, only about seven or eight miles [11 or 13 km] from Delano, my right ankle was swollen like a melon, and the sole of my left foot was just one huge blister.

> Since this was a penitential walk, I refused to take any pain killers. By the time we got to Ducor I was running a temperature. I was so miserable, I thought I was going to die. . . . I went to sleep, but it was just like a short nap before I was awakened at 4:00 in the morning to continue. The pain was severe. . . . My ankle was still swollen. But I marched all that day, about seventeen miles [27 km] to Porterville. By then my leg was swollen up to just below the knee, and my blisters were beginning to bleed on the left foot. . . . The third day was a short march, about twelve miles [19 km]. . . . By then my leg was swollen way up to my thigh, and I was running a high fever.

That evening, as he was preparing to give a speech to the large throng, Chavez received a phone call. The caller identified himself as a lawyer representing Schenley who wanted to negotiate a contract. Chavez thought it was a prank and hung up. The lawyer called back, however, and a meeting was set up the next day in his Beverly Hills home.

Chavez left the march and drove all night to make the meeting. It did not go well at first. At one point, Chavez got up to leave. But eventually he and Schenley's lawyer came to an agreement. If the groups would call off the boycott, the liquor company would recognize the NFWA as the official union of its workers. The company would also provide a union hall and give workers an immediate thirty-five-cent-an-hour raise. Huerta was put in charge of drawing up a full contract, and the two sides agreed to meet again in several months to work out the details.

Chavez rushed back to Sacramento and arrived as the marchers walked into town on Easter Sunday. The crowd swarmed around the steps of the state capitol, and when Chavez announced the news, a

Grape strikers continue the march on April 7, 1966, after they received the good news that Chavez had reached an agreement with Schenley.

Thousands of people gather in Sacramento on April 10, 1966, to join the grape strike marchers in their protest.

raucous cheer went up. Buoyed by the news, Chavez felt the efforts of the strikers would soon pay off. As he told the crowd: "We go back to continue the strike that's lasted now almost seven months with great hopes and expectations that it will not last much longer, and that we, as civilized men, can sit down together with employers."

■ ■ ■ ■ PICKETS AND PRAYERS

The long march placed the Delano grape strike in the national spotlight. But while the Schenley victory was sweet, Chavez knew the other major grower in the region would rather destroy the NFWA than negotiate. DiGiorgio Fruit Corporation, which made more than $231 million in 1965, was virulently antiunion. The company had a long record of using intimidation and violence against workers who tried to organize. During a 1939 strike in Yuba City, DiGiorgio defeated workers with the help of law enforcement officials who beat protesters and ran them out of town.

In 1947 DiGiorgio had used braceros to break a strike. When that failed, the company used its political connections with Richard Nixon, a Republican congressman from California. In 1948 Nixon held congressional hearings about the strike and implied that it was a Communist plot meant to weaken the United States. The strike was finally ended by company violence. Private detectives were hired to fire guns at a union meeting, a move that seriously wounded several people. After this incident, workers were too frightened to attend the meetings.

Nearly two decades later, Chavez knew that fighting DiGiorgio would be very difficult. But he felt he could pressure the company using the same economic weapon that had worked so well against Schenley. Three days after the long march ended in Sacramento, NFWA initiated a boycott against DiGiorgio. Like Schenley, the company produced many well-known brands including S&W Fine Foods and TreeSweet Products. Because the company had made so many enemies among its workforce dating back to the strikes of the 1930s, Chavez was able to mobilize former employees who had not previously joined in the grape strike. These extra people helped the boycott quickly take hold in Chicago, New York, and San Francisco.

The boycott had little effect on DiGiorgio, however, and the company retaliated in its usual way. Private detectives threatened picketers with guns and beat several of them. The pickets and boycott continued for a year, but in May 1967, DiGiorgio obtained an injunction to limit the number of strikers that could march outside its ranch. If the NFWA violated the order, strikers would be arrested and the union would face large fines.

Chavez could not think of a way to get around the injunction, so he called a union meeting to ask for ideas. Three women approached him with a plan. They asked what would happen if people gathered outside the ranch simply to pray. Chavez thought this was brilliant. He rushed home to enlist the help of his brother, Richard. Together they built a small wooden altar that fit in the back of the Chavez's old station wagon. The shrine was decorated with a picture of the Virgin of Guadalupe, candles, and flowers. When the sun rose the next morning, Chavez parked the car with the altar outside DiGiorgio's gates.

The first day, a small group of strikers prayed at the altar until sunset. To increase the crowds, Chavez printed leaflets asking people to attend not a protest but a prayer meeting at DiGiorgio. The event was also announced on Spanish-speaking radio stations in the region. Within days, hundreds of people were praying at the station wagon shrine. Cars were lined up along the road for miles in each direction,

Growers' wives and supporters protest an outdoor mass held by the grape strikers in the 1960s.

and even some of the strikebreakers came to kneel and pray before the Virgin of Guadalupe. Commenting on the great success of the prayer vigil, Chavez said, "Those meetings were responsible in a large part for keeping the spirits up of our people ... [and it] was a beautiful demonstration of the power of nonviolence."

■ A NEW UNION

Chavez knew it would take more than prayer to end the great grape strike. The NFWA desperately needed money to feed the strikers and their families. Many were disheartened and desperate, and quite a few had crossed picket lines to work as scabs for DiGiorgio.

Many observers believed the strike could only be won if the NFWA merged with AWOC to create a more powerful union. This was put to a vote and was widely supported by members of both unions. In July 1966, the two organizations combined to form the United Farm Workers Organizing Committee (UFWOC). In 1972 the name would be shortened to United Farm Workers, or UFW. The executive board of the union elected Chavez as director and Larry Itliong as vice director.

The new union had a budget of ten thousand dollars a month, some of which was provided by the AFL-CIO, the most powerful trade union in the United States. Other donations poured in from fund-raisers, wealthy supporters, and the United Auto Workers. Some of the money was used to purchase 40 acres (16 hectares) of land west of Delano for a union headquarters and service center. Between 1967 and 1969, farmworkers constructed buildings to house union offices, meeting halls, a medical clinic, a farmworkers' retirement home, and a credit union that was managed by Helen Chavez. The buildings included a gasoline and auto service station, where members could buy fuel and have their vehicles repaired. The land, called Forty Acres, also had a small cooperative farm and pasture for cattle to graze. Chavez was able to move into a comfortable office for the first time.

Even before Forty Acres was finished, the influx of money allowed Chavez to think big and expand the strike beyond companies in Delano. The new target was Giumarra Vineyards Corporation, based

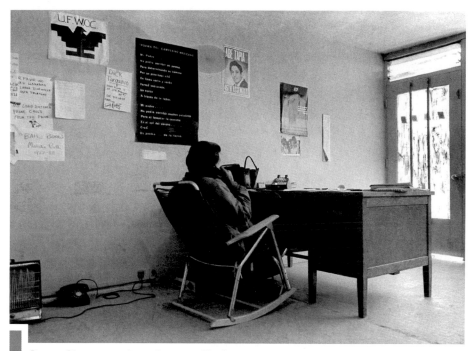

Cesar Chavez makes phone calls from a union office in Salinas, California, in 1970. The merger with AWOC and a budget from the AFL-CIO allowed the UFWOC to build field offices like this.

in Bakersfield, California. Giumarra did not produce grapes for wine. It was the world's largest grower of table grapes, which were sold in grocery stores nationwide. Like DiGiorgio, Giumarra was strongly antiunion and employed tough tactics to keep workers in line. Workers at Giumarra, however, were eager to strike since the company paid lower wages than the rest of the growers in the region.

On August 3, 1967, two-thirds of Giumarra's five thousand workers walked off the job, leaving ripe grapes hanging on the vines. Scabs were brought in, and the company obtained an injunction to prevent strikers from picketing. Rather than fight them in the fields, Chavez decided to enact a nationwide boycott against Giumarra table grapes. Huerta felt this was a tactic for total victory, saying, "If we can crack Giumarra, we can crack them all."

Giumarra developed a new weapon to fight the boycott. Instead of selling grapes under the company name, it used up to one hundred

A strikebreaker picks grapes in Delano in 1966. After getting the grapes picked, growers had to find ways to sell them that avoided the UFWOC-sponsored boycotts.

different labels provided by other growers in California. This move was in violation of federal standards outlined by the Food and Drug Administration. To punish the companies that were helping Giumarra, Huerta convinced UFWOC to extend the boycott to all table grapes grown in California.

Huerta also had a plan to enforce the boycott. She suggested that the union send carloads of picketers to every big city. However, this was impossible with the funds available, so in December 1967, the group rented an old school bus and sent fifty protesters to New York City. They were each paid five dollars a week plus room and board. When the bus arrived, however, it was −5°F (−21°C), and most of the riders had never been out of California's hot Central Valley. As Huerta recalls, there was a problem at the first picket site: "[One] of the Filipino women fell down and hit her head on some ice and had amnesia for about an hour. Everybody was slipping on the ice and falling. But they had a heck of a lot of spirit." Despite the weather, the group succeeded in convincing produce buyers for large markets to stop buying California grapes at New York's main distribution terminal.

The boycott was successful almost immediately. This prompted UFWOC to expand the protests into San Francisco, Boston, Chicago, Los Angeles, and Detroit. To recruit new picketers, organizers fanned out to union halls, churches, and college student lounges. They asked for financial support and signed up people to demonstrate. Protest committees were organized to picket outside large grocery stores and pass out fliers urging customers not to buy California grapes.

As 1967 drew to a close, grape sales were down 12 percent nationwide. This caused some growers to begin negotiations with UFWOC to end the strike. However, a determined majority refused to acknowledge the existence of the union and adamantly opposed any efforts to raise the pay of laborers. This meant that even as the national boycott achieved success, many workers in Delano remained demoralized, downhearted, and penniless.

CHAPTER 5

HUNGER
AND
VICTORY

You and your valiant fellow
workers have demonstrated
your commitment to righting
grievous wrongs forced on
an exploited people."

—Martin Luther King Jr. to Cesar Chavez, telegram, 1968

In early 1968, the great Delano grape strike was more than two years old and the boycott had grown considerably. New volunteers from colleges, churches, and unions were joining the movement and setting up picket lines at big-city supermarkets across the country. As the boycott expanded, even growers who were not involved in the strike decided it was in their interests to sign with UFWOC. For example, major California winemakers including Almadén, Paul Masson, Christian Brothers, and Gallo negotiated labor contracts with Dolores Huerta to avoid becoming boycott targets.

Despite some success, thousands of Mexican American and Filipino farmworkers were still on strike around Delano. There had been little progress against Giumarra and other large growers. And while the strikers in California's Central Valley felt increasingly isolated, they could not help but notice what was happening elsewhere in the nation. U.S. inner-city neighborhoods were filled with anger and frustration. While the nonviolent protests led by Martin Luther King Jr. were helping rural blacks in the South, millions of African Americans living in urban areas were incensed by widespread unemployment, poverty, and racism. In 1965 an incident of police brutality touched off a six-day riot in the Watts area of Los Angeles. By the time the revolt was quelled, 150 square blocks were looted and burned, 34 people were killed, 865 were injured, and 4,000 were arrested. A new chant, "Burn, baby, burn," was born as hundreds watched white-owned businesses and black homes go up in flames. The scene in Watts was repeated in dozens of other U.S. cities in the years that followed.

The televised violence of the big-city riots spawned the Black Power movement. This movement began with SNCC, a group whose members had been working closely with the NFWA for several years in nonviolent protests. In July 1967, however, SNCC leader H. Rap Brown called for nothing less than an armed revolution. Brown told a cheering audience in Maryland: "If America don't come around [to our cause] we going [to] burn it down, brother. We are going to burn it down if we don't get our share of it. . . . Don't love [the white man] to death, shoot him to death."

Above: Fires started during rioting in the Watts neighborhood of Los Angeles fill the sky with smoke in 1965. The riots in Los Angeles and other cities sparked the Black Power movement in the United States. *Below:* H. Rap Brown speaks to a crowd in Maryland in July 1967. Brown's message inspired frustrated Mexican Americans to start a Brown Power movement.

CHICANO POWER

Brown's message resonated with many picketers in Delano. Some of the younger strikers were strongly influenced by urban radicals in the barrios who took their cues from the Black Power movement. These activists began referring to themselves and all Mexican Americans as Chicanos. And their aggressive demands for better pay and equal rights came to be known as Brown Power, or Chicano Power.

The Chicano Power movement was popular with those who were rediscovering their heritage and building a positive sense of self-identity based on *la raza*. The term literally means "the race" but was used to describe all who descended from the Spanish and Indian people of Mexico. The enemy of la raza was said to be the gringo, *gabacho*, or white man. Chavez believed that those who promoted la raza were working against his efforts. He also said it was a racist term meant to demean all others:

> I hear about *la raza* more and more. Some people don't look at it as racism, but when you say *la raza*, you are saying an anti-gringo thing, and our fear is it won't stop there. Today it's anti-gringo, tomorrow it will be anti-Negro, and the day after it will be anti-Filipino, anti-Puerto Rican. And then it will be anti-poor Mexican, and anti-darker-skinned Mexican.

"KILL A FEW OF THEM"

Despite the resistance by Chavez, there was no denying that Chicano Power had come to California's vineyards, orchards, and fields. The young radicals were disdainful of the nonviolent tactics that had guided the grape strike. Some openly accused Chavez of cowardice. Supporters of Chicano Power proclaimed that bloodshed was the only way to convince growers to negotiate. Chavez recalled several strikers saying to him, "Hey, we've got to burn these [growers] down. We've got to kill a few of them."

Such attitudes increased tension on the picket lines, and some strikers began carrying guns. Others openly defied the movement's message of peaceful protest, forming cells and carrying out minor acts of sabotage. Nails were scattered across roads to flatten the tires of police cars and farm trucks. Several grape-filled packing sheds were set on fire, and irrigation pumps were blown up with dynamite.

■ ■ ■ ■ "I STOPPED EATING"

During this time of strife, Chavez recalled the actions of Gandhi. The Indian leader had effectively used hunger strikes on several occasions to draw attention to the peaceful goals of the independence movement. To make a dramatic statement and regain control of the strike, Chavez decided to emulate Gandhi and hold a hunger strike. As he later recalled:

> I had to bring the Movement to a halt, do something that would force them and me to deal with the whole question of violence and ourselves. We had to stop long enough to take account of what we were doing. . . . So I stopped eating. . . . [I] was going to stop eating until such time as everyone in the strike either ignored me or made up their minds that they were not going to be committing violence.

At first Chavez did not make a major announcement about his decision. He simply stopped eating solid food on February 15, 1968. The first day, he walked to Forty Acres and set up a cot in a small storage room in the service station building. This room, resembling a monastic cell (cell of a monk), was next to a larger room that was to be used for an administrative office and chapel.

After four days of drinking only water, Chavez called a meeting and told union members about his fast. Although he usually had strong support among strikers and sympathizers, some were opposed to his new tactic. Helen feared for her husband's health and thought the hunger strike was a crazy idea. Others were contemptuous of the strike's religious implications since fasting was a form of penance promoted by the Catholic Church. However, when news of the hunger strike got out, the majority of farmworkers in the region approved of the fast. Within days, a tent city sprang up in the fields of Forty Acres. Hundreds of people arrived daily to show their support for Chavez, who took part in a nightly mass held for the assembled crowd.

By the second week, Chavez's hunger strike was making national headlines, and supporters were pouring into Delano from across the country. Farmworkers waited in line for hours to talk to the man who was personally sacrificing his health for their benefit. But Chavez was not interested in becoming a martyr or a celebrity. Instead, he used his interactions with the public as a means for spreading the union message. As union spokesman Leroy Chatfield explained:

> Cesar would talk about the workers' home area, he would ask about the conditions there, and then suggest they should try to help themselves, to help form a coordinated effort among the workers, and they would agree. It was like the march [to Sacramento] only different, instead of his going to the people as he did on the march, they came to him.

■ ELOQUENT TESTIMONY TO NONVIOLENCE

On the twenty-first day of the fast, Chavez had to leave Forty Acres to appear in court. Months earlier, Giumarra had obtained an injunction to stop picketing at its ranch, but the union had defied the court order and picketers continued to protest at the vineyard entrance. On February 26, a judge ordered Chavez to personally appear in court and defend the union against these charges. Chavez was extremely weak from hunger, so UFWOC lawyer Jerry Cohen decided to turn the court appearance into a piece of memorable media drama.

The union brought more than one thousand workers to the courthouse on the day of the hearing. The supporters assembled in two long lines from the building's steps, through the front doors, and down the hallway to the courtroom. When Chavez appeared, the protesters fell to their knees and bowed their heads in silent prayer. As cameras rolled, Chatfield and Co-hen propped up the pale Chavez as he walked un-steadily to the courtroom between the rows of defer-ential supporters.

Company owner John-ny Giumarra Jr. was as-tounded at the scene and demanded that the judge order the workers cleared from the courthouse. The judge, however, said, "If I did that it would be just another example of gringo justice." This caused Cohen to comment, "To hear that coming from a Kern Coun-ty judge was something."

In his feeble condition, Chavez was unable to testi-fy, so the judge postponed the proceedings. Several weeks later, Giumarra real-

Leroy Chatfield *(left)* helps Cesar Chavez into court on March 5, 1968. Chavez was on the twenty-first day of his fast when he made his appearance in the Bakersfield court.

ized his company could not win in court and quietly asked the judge to dismiss the case. Picketing at the ranch continued, and the publicity from the court appearance further enlarged the crowds of protesters.

Chavez's hunger strike also attracted the attention of Martin Luther King Jr. On March 5, King sent Chavez a telegram praising his ability to maintain peace during the strike:

> I am deeply moved by your courage in fasting and your personal sacrifice to justice through nonviolence. Your past and present commitment is eloquent testimony to the constructive power of nonviolent action and the destructive impotence of violent

reprisal. You stand today as a living example of [Gandhian] tradition with its great force for social progress and its healing spiritual powers.... The plight of your people and ours is so grave that we all desperately need the inspiring example and effective leadership you have given.

On March 10, 1968, the twenty-five-day fast came to an end at a service in a Delano park attended by more than six thousand people. Robert Kennedy was invited to speak, and when he arrived, he was mobbed by farmworkers who tried to kiss him, touch him, and shake his hand. After an ecumenical service conducted by ministers, rabbis, priests, and nuns, Kennedy gave a rousing speech advocating rights for farm laborers. Chavez was too frail to speak, so an aide read a prepared statement:

I am convinced that the truest act of courage, the strongest act of manliness, is to sacrifice ourselves for others in a totally nonviolent struggle for justice. To be a man is to suffer for others. God help us be men.

On March 10, 1968, thousands of people, including Dolores Huerta *(center)*, Larry Itliong *(second from right)*, and Robert Kennedy *(right)* rallied to Cesar Chavez's cause and turned out to see him break his fast.

Finally, with dozens of news cameras clicking away, Kennedy and Chavez shared a small piece of bread. Soon after, Chavez was carried to a mattress in the back of a station wagon and taken home to recover. His fast had lasted longer than Gandhi's famous 1924 hunger strike, he had lost 30 pounds (14 kg), and his muscles were degenerating from lack of food. Still, Chavez had made his point. There was an almost unanimous feeling among strikers that nonviolence was the only way to win.

Cesar Chavez *(right)* and Robert Kennedy *(center)* share a piece of bread to break Chavez's fast in 1968. Chavez's wife, Helen, is at left.

■ ■ ■ POLITICAL TRAGEDIES

The drama of the hunger strike also served to inspire Kennedy. Although many people urged him to run for president after his brother was assassinated in 1963, the senator had never said that he would. But on the way back to the airport after breaking bread with Chavez, Kennedy told an UFWOC leader in the car that he intended to run for president. This was the first time he made this pronouncement, and a week later, he officially declared his intention at a national news conference.

Although UFWOC resources were stretched to the limit, union members could not resist helping the senator who had walked the picket line with them in Delano. Analysts believed that if a majority of Chicano voters cast their ballot for Kennedy in the California June primary, he would win the Democratic nomination in August and inevitably be elected president in November. This inspired union volunteers to spread out through big city barrios and small farm towns to convince Chicanos to vote in the primary.

The move to get Kennedy elected became more urgent on April 4, 1968, when Martin Luther King Jr. was assassinated in Memphis, Tennessee, while helping sanitation workers organize there. Despite his message of nonviolence, King's death sparked bloody riots in more than one hundred U.S. cities, including Washington, D.C.; Los Angeles; Chicago; and Baltimore. Indianapolis was one of the few cities that did not experience violence. Kennedy was attending a campaign rally there, and against the wishes of his security staff, he drove to the inner city where he spoke eloquently to an angry, frustrated crowd:

> What we need in the United States is not division; what we need in the United States is not hatred; what we need in the United States is not violence and lawlessness, but love and wisdom, and compassion toward one another, and a feeling of justice toward those who still suffer within our country, whether they be white or whether they be black.

Although Kennedy did not mention Mexican Americans, his message resonated with Chicano voters. They turned out in record numbers

After Martin Luther King Jr. was assassinated, Cesar Chavez wrote an editorial in *El Malcriado* linking the slain civil rights leader to the farmworkers' movement:

> There is a bond between the struggle of the farm workers in California and Dr. Martin Luther King, Jr. It is a bond of love and leadership, a bond which cannot be broken by the bullet of his assassin. It was Dr. Martin Luther King who taught us to value ourselves as individuals. His example proved for us that all farm workers, Mexicans, Filipinos, Negroes, Anglos, could live together and work together to gain the place in society which we merit as men. Dr. King proved that the only road we can walk is that of non-violence and love. It was his example that inspired and continues to inspire us as we confront the obstacles on that road, and overcome them. . . . The victories achieved under his leadership were no less important for the poor in the fields of our nation than for the poor in the cities.

for the California primary, ensuring Kennedy's victory. In some Chicano voting districts, the senator received 100 percent of the vote.

A victory celebration was held in the ballroom at the Ambassador Hotel in Los Angeles. Cesar and Helen Chavez were in attendance along with Huerta and other members of UFWOC. After Kennedy addressed supporters in the early morning hours of June 5, he exited the ballroom through the kitchen. In the push of the crowd, a twenty-four-year-old

Palestinian named Sirhan Sirhan approached Kennedy from behind and shot him three times in the back of the head. Kennedy died the next day. Sirhan knew little about California grape workers. He was upset by Kennedy's support of the Jewish state of Israel.

■ A DARK CLOUD

Kennedy's senseless assassination cast a dark cloud over the grape strike. Many felt Kennedy would have easily won in November. Instead, Republican Richard Nixon was elected. Nixon, who had once called grape strikers Communists, had been a recipient of DiGiorgio campaign contributions for more than two decades. When he was running for president, he often gave speeches denouncing the grape strike and the boycott.

Nixon was not the only powerful Republican who opposed UFWOC efforts. Former movie star Ronald Reagan had been sworn in as California governor in 1967 after defeating Democrat Edmund "Pat" Brown, who was sympathetic to the strikers. Reagan often made a point of eating grapes in public to show his support for the growers. Reagan also demonstrated his commitment to agribusiness by appointing Allan Grant to head the California Board of Agriculture, the government agency that investigated complaints filed by Chavez. Previously Grant had been president of the California Farm Bureau Federation, an organization dominated

Richard Nixon *(right)* and Ronald Reagan *(left)* campaign in California in 1968. The two Republicans, Nixon as U.S. president and Reagan as California governor, backed the growers in the ongoing labor battles between growers and farmworkers.

by major growers. As head of the Board of Agriculture, he stated the grape boycott was "the most serious crisis that California agriculture has ever faced. It has developed into the ultimate confrontation. . . . [It is] immoral, unethical, and reprehensible. . . . [The UFWOC] is trying to blackmail California."

With few allies in high political office in California or Washington, D.C., UFWOC could no longer count on sympathetic officials to help the cause. In fact, Nixon deliberately worked to harm the strikers. The president ordered the Defense Department to buy up California grapes and use them to feed soldiers who were fighting in Vietnam. In 1969 the military had increased its purchase of grapes to 11 million pounds (5 million kg) a year, nearly double the 1968 amount. Even so, there were reports of Chicano sailors supporting the strike by throwing boxes of California grapes into the sea.

Nixon's orders came at a time when Chavez was faltering in his leadership position. He had been severely weakened by the twenty-five-day fast, and in early September 1968, he was stricken with such severe back pain that he had to be hospitalized. Doctors could not determine what was wrong, but some thought he had permanently injured his spine. Rumors circulated that Chavez had cancer.

Chavez was hospitalized until February 1969. He was able to conduct union business from his bed, but the agony was worse than the pain of the Sacramento march or even the hunger strike. Chavez considered his situation hopeless until a doctor discovered something during a routine exam. One of Chavez's legs was slightly shorter than the other, a condition that caused his spine to twist. After receiving physical therapy, Chavez was able to walk without pain for the first time in years.

"GET THAT SUPPORT"

While Chavez was bedridden, the grape boycott continued. Between 1968 and 1969, picketers were targeting supermarkets in almost fifty cities. Huerta oversaw the national movement, sending one or two farmworker families to each of the cities. These people supervised volunteers from all walks of life. Huerta explained her tactics:

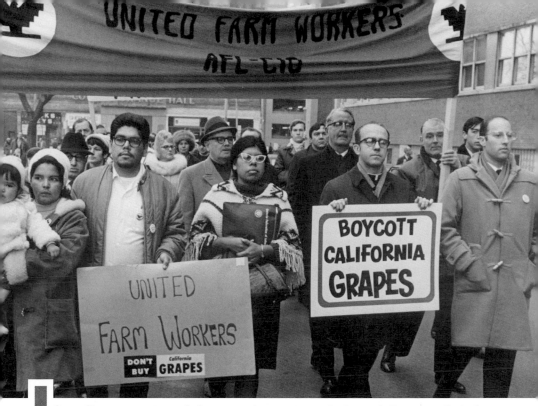

Canadian supporters of the grape boycott march through Toronto, Ontario, in December 1968.

The whole thrust of our boycott is to get as many supporters involved as you can. You have to get organizers who can go to the unions, to the churches, to the students and get that support. You divide an area up—in New York we split it up into eight sections. We get supporters to help us picket and leaflet; we go after one chain at a time, telling the shoppers where they can find other stores.

Maintaining the boycott was expensive, costing UFWOC up to forty thousand dollars a month. With no money to pay salaries, every union worker, including Huerta and Chavez, was paid five dollars a week plus expenses. Those who traveled stayed at churches, homes of volunteers, or what were called boycott houses. These were usually old run-down houses owned by churches or temples. Most were located in crime-infested inner-city neighborhoods.

Investigative reporter Ronald B. Taylor participated in the grape boycott in 1969. In his book, *Chavez and the Farm Workers*, he describes the accommodations known as boycott houses where the picketers stayed in various cities:

> The Boston [Massachusetts] boycott house was a big, old, gray three-story rectory [living quarters for religious workers] that once served a Catholic church next door. It is in the heart of a black ghetto, and the building has had little care since it was abandoned by the church and donated to the union cause. The house has seven bedrooms and three bathrooms, in various states of disrepair. What formerly was the front sitting room has been converted into a workroom and print shop, while the large dining room and kitchen have retained their original functions. The 10 to 15 boycott people living in the house rotate the cooking and housekeeping chores. Because of the racial tension in Boston everyone who was white was warned about walking the streets alone at night. Two of the volunteers had been robbed at knife point a few days before I arrived.

> The boycott house in Jersey City [New Jersey] is almost a duplicate of the one in Boston, except it is located on the dividing line between Puerto Rican and black neighborhoods. Violence and burglary are common occurrences; the Jersey City boycotters have lost duplicating machines, movie projectors, and tape recorders in a series of thefts.

THE CONSUMER RIGHTS COMMITTEE

As the boycott continued, grape growers were forced to admit that the strike was taking its toll on business. The boycott was the subject of a *Time* magazine cover story that portrayed farmworkers in a very sympathetic manner. This helped spread the movement beyond liberal households, union members, and students to encompass middle-class buyers in the United States and Canada.

Growers and agribusiness associations realized that it was imperative to stage a unified battle against UFWOC with money, politicians, and public relations campaigns. The California Farm Bureau Federation led the way. The organization convinced California senator George Murphy to introduce legislation that would outlaw strikes during harvest season and make boycotts illegal. The bill would also give agribusiness interests favorable treatment when the government mediated disputes between laborers and growers.

Grape producers also backed a million-dollar campaign to boost the image of growers in California. They hired a conservative San Francisco-based public relations firm to mount a PR battle against the boycott. The firm devised the slogan "consumer rights" and formed the Consumer Rights Committee, which set up offices in cities where the boycott was active. The committee put forth the message that supermarkets had no right to keep grapes off their shelves since some consumers wanted to buy them. They said the public had the right to choose what it wanted to eat. President Nixon supported the campaign and gave a speech in San Francisco in which he falsely claimed the boycott was illegal.

Delano growers also set up an organization to fight the boycott. The Agricultural Workers Freedom to Work Association (AWFWA) was populated by growers, labor contractors, and field bosses who had been exploiting farmworkers for decades. Despite its membership, AWFWA presented itself as a workers' rights association. The group released a statement explaining its function was "to tell workers not to be afraid of Chavez, to be united . . . [because AWFWA] would support and protect the workers; we [are] opposed to UFWOC efforts to organize and boycott . . . and [we] try to enlist workers."

AWFWA paid representatives to give speeches in boycott cities. The speakers said that grape workers in Delano were not on strike and that most field-workers did not support the boycott. AWFWA representatives never mentioned that most of these laborers in the field were scabs.

■ ■ ■ ■ POISONED GRAPES

Although the public relations campaigns did little to improve grape sales, most growers adamantly refused to give in to union demands. Feeling that the boycott battle had become a stalemate, lawyer Jerry Cohen began searching for a new legal strategy to fight the growers. In the summer of 1969, he found a new line of attack in the complaints that grape workers filed with UFWOC about the use of pesticides in the vineyards. The union was able to use this discovery to create dramatic negative publicity for California grape growers.

Several dozen workers had complained that they were being poisoned by pesticides. The pesticides were making them nauseous and causing blisters on their skin. Growers distributed the poisons in unmarked containers, so workers did not know what sort of chemicals they were using. Cohen began investigating and discovered growers were required by state law to register any pesticide they used with the county agricultural commission. The commission refused to reveal information about pesticide use to Cohen, saying it was a confidential trade secret.

Cohen refused to accept that the county agricultural commissioners had the final word on this important matter. He filed a lawsuit against them, and while studying the issue, he discovered some shocking information. For several years, growers had been using an extremely toxic chemical called Aldrin, which attacked the central nervous system of insects. One drop of Aldrin in its undiluted form could kill a human being within minutes. Workers mixed the chemical with water before spraying it on grape vines and leaves. They absorbed the chemical into their skin while mixing and spraying the chemical. Exposure to the pesticide caused serious physical maladies including dizziness, rashes, nausea, vision and respiratory problems, and cancer.

A farmer sprays pesticide in a vineyard. Pesticides had long been in use when Chavez brought to light the dangers to farmworkers from pesticides.

Boycotters in Washington, D.C., heard about Cohen's investigation. They purchased some California grapes from a grocery store and had the fruit analyzed in a laboratory. Tests revealed that the grapes' levels of Aldrin residue were far higher than allowed by the Food and Drug Administration (FDA). This information eventually led the FDA to ban the use of Aldrin. Before the government could take action, though, boycotters spread the word that California table grapes were poisonous and could cause cancer. Within days, sales of grapes dropped sharply. Safeway, the largest retailer of California produce, was forced to issue a statement saying its grapes contained low levels of pesticide residue and were safe to eat.

SHORT, SWEET VICTORY

The Aldrin issue began an ongoing debate over the safety of pesticide residue on produce. Chavez, though, was less concerned with consumers than with farmworkers, who were forced to spend long days covered in Aldrin and other poisonous chemicals. He told a U.S. senate subcommittee that the use of pesticides had become a more important issue than that of worker wages and benefits. In the aftermath of the investigation, Huerta began including language in labor contracts that required growers to provide safety equipment and Spanish warning labels on pesticide containers.

The pesticide scare was another blow against the growers, and one of the farmers in the Coachella Valley was ready to concede. Lionel Steinberg owned the biggest vineyard in the region, and in April 1970, he said he would sign a contract. Steinberg only had one condition. He wanted the proceedings mediated by a special committee that the National Conference of Catholic Bishops had set up to help arbitrate the dispute.

Residents of Miami, Florida, picket outside of a grocery store in September 1969. The boycott regained momentum in the summer of 1969 when the UFWOC began proclaiming the dangers of pesticides.

Cesar Chavez *(left)* shakes hands with Lionel Steinberg, a Coachella Valley grape grower, after the two announced a contract for farmworkers in April 1970.

After Steinberg signed a contract with UFWOC, he was pleasantly surprised to discover that his grapes were in high demand. Seven major supermarkets in Canada put in orders for Steinberg's union-labeled fruit. This pushed several more major growers into signing with UFWOC, including those who had violently opposed the strike. Then, on July 25, Johnny Giumarra Jr. called Cohen and asked for a contract. Cohen agreed but added one condition. He wanted Giumarra to convince the other twenty-six grape growers in Delano to sign with the union. Giumarra agreed, and the next day, Chavez, Huerta, Itliong, and Cohen met with a large group of bishops, growers, and their lawyers at Forty Acres. The negotiations were long and arduous, lasting well into the next day, but a contract was finally approved by all parties. The union was victorious.

It was agreed that the growers would grant an immediate pay raise to $1.65 an hour, which would increase to $1.80 in a few months. In addition, workers would receive 25¢ for every box packed in the field. The contract further stipulated that a joint committee of union members and growers would be formed to regulate pesticide use. The employers would also pay 10¢ an hour per worker into the union's Robert F. Kennedy Health and Welfare Plan. This plan would provide medical care and financial assistance to farmworkers. Finally, the farmworkers would receive a few things that meant so much in the fields, such as fresh water and clean, accessible bathrooms.

Johnny Guimarra Jr. holds a copy of the union label that his family would use at their vineyard after signing a contract with the United Farm Workers in 1970. Cesar Chavez *(seated, left)* represented the United Farm Workers in the negotiations.

"If the grower wanted to negotiate, things moved pretty fast, but if they didn't want to negotiate, then the talks dragged out like Christian Brothers [brandy producers]. They were very difficult, and this is where persistence pays off, you just have to keep hammering away. You may have to have five meetings to change two words. . . . This is where Cesar gets uptight. He never really quite trusted what I did until he started to negotiate himself; then he found it was pretty hard to get the kind of language that I had gotten [in the contracts], and he started respecting what I had done."

—Dolores Huerta, 1975

The contract brought the long-running labor dispute to an end, and everyone seemed happy that it was over. Giumarra called the strike an experiment in social justice and a revolution in agriculture. Chavez did not gloat but continued to stress the spiritual benefits of nonviolent protest: "The strikers and the people involved in this struggle sacrificed a lot, sacrificed all their worldly possessions. Ninety-five percent of the strikers lost their homes and their cars. But I think in losing those worldly possessions they found themselves." After the contract was signed, about 85 percent of all grapes in California were harvested by UFWOC members. The remaining 15 percent were produced by small family growers who did not use migrant labor.

For Chavez, the victory was sweet but short. There was trouble in the lettuce fields of Salinas Valley, where nonunion workers were threatening to strike. Immediately after Chavez signed the contract ending the Delano grape strike, he rushed off to Salinas to continue fighting for farmworkers. A major battle had been won, but the war in the fields was still raging.

CHAPTER 6

A MIXED
LEGACY

Cesar has died in peace with a serene look on his face. It was as if he had chosen to die . . . at this Easter time. . . . He died so that we would wake up. He died so that the union might live."

—Dolores Huerta, spoken at Cesar Chavez's funeral, April 1993

■ ■ ■ During the late 1960s, the United States' attention was focused on the great Delano Grape Strike. But unseen by most people were the thousands of farmworkers toiling in California's strawberry fields, avocado orchards, and lettuce rows. The conditions these people faced every day had improved little since the 1930s. Many of these laborers had quietly joined the United Farm Workers Organizing Committee during the grape strike, expecting the union to help them organize their own walkouts and boycotts. But Chavez asked them to wait until the grape strike was won. And wait they did. The strawberry workers in the Central Coast city of Santa Maria first wanted to strike in 1967. Those in the Imperial Valley lettuce fields wanted to strike in 1968. By 1970 many had come down with strike fever.

Because of the commitments Chavez made to those farmworkers, he put others in charge of implementing the UFWOC contract in Delano. Low-paid workers needed to create an administration that would oversee the complex day-to-day needs of union members. UFWOC would have to deal with medical insurance, immigration status, Social Security, and countless other details for up to twenty thousand workers. This was an enormously difficult task, and Chavez would not be there to help them because of the promises he had made to workers in Salinas.

■ ■ ■ TEAMSTERS TAKEOVER

The Salinas Valley, located along the Central Coast in California, is known as the Salad Bowl of the World, for the lettuce, broccoli, mushrooms, and numerous other produce crops grown there. In August and September 1970, thousands of migrant workers went on strike in the valley. Their grievances were typical for farmworkers—low pay, terrible working and living conditions, and exposure to dangerous pesticides. But their strike was complicated by the fact that another union was involved. This union was brought in specifically to oppose UFWOC.

When the growers in Salinas viewed the success Chavez was having with the grape strike and boycott, they took steps to halt his influence in their region. The ranchers asked the Teamsters Union to represent Salinas farmworkers, and the union signed contracts that covered thousands of field hands. The laborers themselves were not told about this arrangement until it was completed. Although farmworkers were not included in negotiations, those who did not want to honor the union contracts—and pay union dues to the Teamsters—were fired.

In 1970 the International Brotherhood of Teamsters (IBT) was one of the most powerful and influential labor unions in the United States. The union represented the majority of the nation's truck drivers, cannery and warehouse workers, and other blue-collar laborers. But the Teamsters had close ties to organized crime. Teamster bosses engaged in bribery, embezzlement, extortion, beatings, and bombings to control trucking and related industries. Politicians and police were paid large bribes to look the other way.

The Teamsters were also closely associated with President Nixon. Although the union traditionally backed Democrats, Nixon courted Teamster president Frank Fitzsimmons, who gave the union's endorsement to Nixon when he was running for reelection in 1972.

Although the Teamsters sought to control a large portion of the U.S. workforce, they had previously shown little interest in farmworkers. But in making a deal with thirty Salinas ranchers, the Teamsters added more than eleven thousand farm laborers to their union overnight. And the IBT clearly sided with the growers by viewing Chavez and UFWOC as an enemy to be destroyed.

When growers in other regions saw what was happening in Salinas, they too wanted to sign with the Teamsters. Soon the IBT was signing up farmworkers on 175 ranches along the Central Coast, the Imperial Valley, the San Joaquin Valley, and western Arizona. This move meant that the clout of the Teamsters was coupled with some of the most powerful multinational corporations in the world. The nation's major lettuce producer, Freshpict Corporation, was owned by Purex, the household name in bleach during the 1960s. Pic N Pac, the largest grower of strawberries in the world, was owned by Boston gourmet food producer S. S. Pierce. And the vegetable firm InterHarvest was a subsidiary of United Fruit, a company with a notorious reputation for

Frank Fitzsimmons *(right)* was the Teamster president in 1970. He had taken over for Jimmy Hoffa *(left)* after Hoffa was convicted of attempted bribery of a grand juror. The Teamsters were brought in by the growers to be an alternative union to the UFWOC. The Teamsters viewed Chavez and the UFWOC as enemies in labor battles.

supporting brutal dictatorships in Latin America. Its board members were responsible for backing plots that deposed democratically elected leaders in Guatemala and elsewhere.

Chavez had not planned on battling the giants of corporate America, let alone the Teamsters. But he knew that if he failed to step in, UFWOC would lose tens of thousands of potential members throughout California and Arizona. As Chavez stated, "They can't get away with this. It's preposterous. They're going to have a big fight on their hands. . . . They're not going to sign up our people."

Most farmworkers agreed with Chavez. They had overwhelmingly supported the grape strike and were deeply loyal to UFWOC. Many even called themselves Chavistas—ardent supporters of Chavez and la causa. When the laborers discovered the Teamsters were making secret deals with ranchers, they understood it was done to prevent strikes in the fields.

"A NEW AGE, A NEW ERA"

To protest the actions by the Teamsters and the growers, UFWOC planned a rally on August 2, 1970, at the Hartnell Community College football field in Salinas. In a move reminiscent of the long march to Sacramento, farmworkers from small towns throughout the valley began marching to Salinas. On the day of the gathering, more than three thousand Chavistas paraded down the city's main street chanting "Huelga," some wearing the brown berets of the Chicano Power movement.

Hartnell stadium was filled with a sea of black and red UFWOC banners, Mexican and U.S. flags, and pictures of the Virgin of Guadalupe and Martin Luther King Jr. In a fiery speech, Chavez compared the Teamsters' actions to the surprise attack by the Japanese air force on the U.S. Navy at Pearl Harbor in 1941. He told farmworkers to refuse to sign Teamster union cards. And he threatened growers with a new boycott of their most popular products, including United Fruit's Chiquita bananas and Purex's Dutch cleanser.

Near the end of the speech, Chavez brought up the explosive issue of race. The membership of the Teamsters union was largely white, as were the corporate officers of the food producers who dominated the region. Chavez said, "It's tragic that these men have not yet come to understand that we are in a new age, a new era. No longer can a couple of white men sit together and write the destinies of all the Chicanos and Filipino workers in this valley."

THE UNITED FARM WORKERS OF AMERICA

On August 23, 1970, workers in Salinas went on strike. Tensions were high, and Chavez undertook a six-day fast to calm the situation. This had little effect on the Teamsters, however, and the IBT employed the tactics that had made it the most powerful and feared union in the United States. Teamster thugs showed up at picket lines with baseball bats, chains, and shotguns. Protesters were attacked and severely beaten as police stood by and did nothing. Cohen was punched and kicked in the face and ended up in the hospital with a concussion.

Cesar Chavez *(right)* talks to UFWOC picketers and reminds them to be peaceful during strikes in the Salinas Valley in 1970.

Teamsters also planted dynamite at the UFWOC office in Hollister, California, blowing out the windows and doors in a late-night explosion. Unlike the Delano strike, this time strikers fought back. Three were arrested for shooting and wounding a Teamster organizer in Santa Maria, California. For the first time, serious bloodshed was making headlines during a farmworkers' strike.

In November ranchers obtained injunctions to stop UFWOC picketing. When strikers continued to protest, a judge jailed Chavez indefinitely until the injunction was obeyed. Thousands of protesters set up a round-the-clock vigil at the jail, while police made sporadic arrests for trespassing. But things threatened to get out of hand on December 6, when Ethel Kennedy came to offer her support to Chavez. The widow of the assassinated senator was greeted by jeering Teamsters, who yelled obscenities, shoved supporters, and threatened to attack her. This incited UFWOC supporters to fight back, and there were fears that a riot would break out. Somehow, violence was averted, and Chavez was released on Christmas Eve after the California Supreme Court ruled the injunctions were unconstitutional.

Observers thought the Salinas strike, like the one in Delano, might stretch out for five years. But it soon appeared that the growers had underestimated the power of UFWOC. United Fruit, in particular, was sensitive to boycott threats because so many Americans already held the company in contempt for its vicious political tactics in Central America. The company was afraid that if people stopped buying its Chiquita bananas, they would never start again. This prompted United Fruit to rescind the InterHarvest contract with the Teamsters. As part of the deal, UFWOC workers would be given a raise from $1.75 an hour to $2.15. Piece rates for each carton packed would be raised to 11¢. Within weeks Freshpict and Pic N Pac conceded defeat. This prompted smaller growers in the region to sign with UFWOC.

After the 1970s strike was settled, UFWOC membership grew to eighty thousand. With so many new members, the union was forced to leave its Forty Acres headquarters and move to a new complex in La Paz, south of Bakersfield. In 1972 UFWOC became independently affiliated with the AFL-CIO and changed its name to the United Farm Workers of America (UFW).

"THE SPIRIT OF FEAR"

The union had prevailed once again, but the lessons of the past were hard to ignore. Chavez had been reluctant to go on strike in 1965 because he had seen that gains from previous strikes were only temporary. Once the pressure was off, growers would do whatever they could to cut costs and deny farmworkers their rights. And this proved true throughout the rest of the 1970s, when the UFW was forced to revisit the same battles over and over as food producers used their money and power to push back against the union.

Above: Supporters of Cesar Chavez demonstrate outside of a barber shop in Salinas, California. The signs translate to "freedom for Chavez." Chavez had been imprisoned because picketers had ignored a judge's order to call off a strike.

Right: Ethel Kennedy *(in black coat),* the wife of assassinated senator Robert Kennedy, joins Larry Itliong *(bottom right)* and others in protest of Chavez's imprisonment in December 1970. The group is marching to the jail where he was held.

In 1972 agribusiness interests spent millions of dollars to make changes in labor laws that favored big growers. Rather than worry about boycotts and picketing, they worked with state legislatures in California, Arizona, and other farm states to strictly regulate UFW activities. While the union was able to stop the regulations in some places, Arizona passed stiff laws that severely restricted farmworkers' rights. Consumer boycotts were outlawed, and protesters could be arrested simply for telling people not to buy Arizona lettuce. If the union wanted to hold a strike, it had to take part in a lengthy process with a Labor Relations Board, whose members were appointed by the Republican governor. In the unlikely event that the board authorized a strike, growers could ask for a six-month cooling-off period before the action could proceed.

In reaction to the Arizona law, Chavez decided to hold a hunger strike in Phoenix on May 30, 1972. In an open letter announcing the fast, Chavez wrote, "My major concern is not this particular Arizona law.... My concern is the spirit of fear that lies behind such laws in the hearts of growers and legislators across the country. Somehow these powerful men and women must be helped to realize that there is nothing to fear from treating their workers as fellow human beings."

During his 1972 hunger strike, Cesar Chavez *(front, second from right)* attends a memorial for Robert F. Kennedy with Kennedy's son, Joseph *(left)* and folksinger Joan Baez *(right)*.

In May 1972, Chavez began another hunger strike. In an open letter to supporters, he questioned why growers and politicians in Arizona were trying to pass laws against boycotting and calling strikes during harvest season:

Dear Brothers and Sisters:

Our people have been poor for more years than we can remember. We have made only a small amount of progress these past ten years of work and struggle. Our women and children still die too often and too young. There is too much hunger and disease among us. Not even 5 percent of America's migrant farm workers are protected by union contracts. Yet there is a great fear of our union—a fear that I do not fully understand, but that I know is present with most growers and especially among the lettuce growers in the current resistance to the rights of their workers. Growers through the Farm Bureau are seeking to bring the whole machinery of government against us. Why are they so afraid of a union for migrant farm workers? Is it so much to ask that the poorest people of the land have a measure of justice? . . . What is it that causes sane men to act so hastily and so cruelly? It cannot be that we are so powerful. In the context of the great corporations, we are like a mosquito on an elephant's back.

Cesar Chavez's second fast in 1972 produced one of the movement's most lasting slogans. Before Chavez began the fast, many advisers told him he could not survive another punishing physical ordeal. They said in Spanish, "No *se puede, no se puede*" (It can't be done). But supporters of the fast retaliated, "*Sí! se puede!*" (Yes, it can be done!). The English translation of the slogan, "Yes we can!" was adopted by Barack Obama when he ran for the U.S. Senate as a Democrat from Illinois in 2004, and it was the slogan of his successful 2008 presidential campaign.

PROTECTED BY LAW

Chavez suffered more during his second hunger strike than he had during the first. He was now forty-five years old, and his body was worn down from years of marches, sixteen-hour workdays, and long periods without food. In Phoenix he lost the ability to hold down water, his heartbeat was erratic, and he was in and out of the hospital. He broke the fast after twenty-four days at a mass attended by five thousand people, but he was extremely sick during the event.

The hunger strike did little to stop growers from fighting the union. In 1973 Delano ranchers refused to renew the three-year contract they had hammered out with UFWOC after the grape strike. Instead, they signed with the Teamsters without holding a worker election. In protest, union members in the Coachella and San Joaquin valleys walked out on strike. And once again, ranchers reacted with injunctions, mass arrests, beatings, and shootings that left two dead. Growing violence forced Chavez to call off the strike after three months and begin a second grape boycott.

The televised images of bloody strikers made a strong impression on the American public and helped gain support for the boycott. By

Grower John Giumarra *(center)* talks to picketers in 1973. Shortly after Giumarra left, sheriff deputies attacked the picketers in an attempt to break the strike.

1974 a Louis Harris poll confirmed that seventeen million consumers were boycotting California grapes, lettuce, and Gallo wine.

In November 1974, California underwent a political shift that proved beneficial to the UFW. Democrat Jerry Brown was elected governor when Reagan's term ended. Brown was a labor law specialist who had met with Chavez on several occasions and had supported the farmworkers' cause since the 1960s.

After Brown took office, he held extended meetings with growers, Teamsters, UFW lawyers, and politicians to create peace between the warring parties. The final result was a law called the Agriculture Labor Relations Act passed by the California legislature in June. This landmark bill secured unprecedented rights for the state's farmworkers. The goal of the act was "to ensure peace in the fields of California by guaranteeing justice for all agricultural workers and stability in

California governor Jerry Brown *(second from left)* walks with Cesar Chavez *(second from right)* in the 1970s. Brown was the first California governor in many years who supported the labor causes of Chavez and the UFW.

agricultural labor relations. The Board seeks to achieve these ends by providing orderly processes for protecting, implementing, and enforcing the respective rights and responsibilities of employees, employers and labor organizations in their relations with each other."

The act gave farmworkers the freedom to pick representatives of their own choosing, which would prevent unwanted representation by the Teamsters. It allowed them to negotiate the terms and conditions of their employment free from interference by growers or outside unions. The new law also created the California Agricultural Labor Relations Board (ALRB), a government agency charged with overseeing union elections and investigating unfair labor practices. When Brown signed the bill into law, he gave the UFW new powers and a legitimacy that had taken decades of struggle to achieve.

"A CRUEL HOAX"

In 1976 the ALRB monitored more than eighty union elections. In each one, farmworkers overwhelmingly rejected the IBT and chose the UFW to represent them, expanding union membership to twenty thousand. Within two years, the Teamsters would give up on their quest to represent field-workers in California. As in earlier years, however, the growers refused to accept union victories, choosing instead to fight back.

California agribusiness growers pursued two strategies to reduce the power of the UFW. First, they used their political influence over rural legislators to reduce funding to the ALRB. This made it very difficult for the agency to carry out its duties, which included monitoring dozens of union elections and investigating unfair labor practices. In addition, growers hired teams of skilled lawyers to challenge nearly every unfavorable decision made by the board. This meant agency personnel had to appear in court to defend decisions, an expensive and time-consuming procedure. As a result of this two-pronged attack, the ALRB did not have enough staff to enforce the Agriculture Labor Relations Act. Growers could continue to fire and blacklist union organizers, disrupt union elections with thugs, or simply ignore union demands.

By 1977 Chavez was disillusioned and disheartened. The Agriculture Labor Relations Act that he had fought to implement was completely ineffective. As he stated, "Most farmworkers have yet to realize the promise and protection of this good law. Instead, for the most, the law has been a cruel hoax."

■ NO TRUE DEMOCRACY

The string of defeats in the late 1970s drove a rift between the leaders of the UFW. Although millions of people saw Chavez as a saintlike figure, many union officers felt that their hard work was being ignored. There was also racial tension between Filipino union members and the Mexican Americans, who were in the majority. In 1977 this caused UFW vice president and highest-ranking Filipino officer Philip Vera Cruz to quit. He later commented that non-Chicanos felt nearly invisible in the union, citing UFW slogans as an example:

When [Mexican Americans] called out "Viva La Raza," or "Viva

Cesar Chavez," they didn't realize all these vivas did not include the Filipinos. As a matter of fact they didn't include anyone else but themselves. That, of course, turned off many Filipinos and the other smaller minorities within the union, like the Blacks and Arabs. The Filipinos especially didn't like it when the [Chicanos] referred to themselves as "*Chavistas*." Terms not inclusive but divisive.

Vera Cruz believed that the union suffered because many members idolized Chavez and viewed him as indispensable and even invincible. Union members were not allowed to criticize their leader in public, and this led to the union making some bad decisions. As Vera Cruz stated, "If a union leader is built up as a symbol and he talks like he was God, then there is no way you can have true democracy in the union because the members are just generally deprived of their right to reason for themselves."

CANCER CLUSTERS

Despite such sentiments, the UFW continued to grow in the 1980s. Although the ALRB had been a disappointment, the UFW had more than one hundred thousand members. By sheer numbers alone, the union was able to force growers to accede to many of its demands. Backed by tough labor contracts hammered out by Huerta and Cohen, some union lettuce pickers were earning several times the minimum wage, which was $3.10 an hour at the time. The workers were also provided vacation pay, medical insurance, and other benefits that were unimaginable during the 1960s. But the difficult nature of stoop labor had changed little during the decades of struggle, and workers were still exposed to deadly poisons on a daily basis.

Although Aldrin had been banned in 1969, similar chemicals remained in widespread usage. By the 1980s, growers were using 2.6 million tons (2.3 million metric tons) of pesticides annually. According to government figures, more than three hundred thousand people were sickened by these chemicals every year. Many of the victims were farmworkers, who were experiencing a wide variety of medical problems, such as cancer, sterility, and birth defects.

Airplanes sprayed fields with pesticides that sometimes rained down on farmworkers who were not first warned to leave the area. On occasion accidental sprayings could affect hundreds of men, women, and children at a time. Rural hospitals in agricultural communities would be overwhelmed by people who were drooling, vomiting, and experiencing low heart rates. The short-term effects of pesticide exposure were usually treatable. But those who studied the problem noticed a greater-than-expected number of cancer cases, or cancer clusters, around farm towns.

The UFW increased its focus on pesticides after Dr. Marion Moses began studying cancer clusters in the Central Valley. Moses first joined the union as a volunteer nurse during the Delano grape strike. She studied to become a doctor at the urging of Chavez. When she began interviewing farmworkers in 1983, Moses was shocked to discover unusually high incidences of childhood leukemia, an exceedingly rare disease in most communities.

■ THE GRAPES OF WRATH BOYCOTT

Moses's work inspired Chavez to initiate the Grapes of Wrath boycott, named after the John Steinbeck novel that told the stories of migrant farmworkers during the Depression. The third grape boycott began on June 12, 1984, when millions of computer-generated mailers were sent out warning consumers of a public health hazard associated with pesticides. The union urged people not to eat grapes until five chemicals suspected of causing cancer in laboratory animals were banned.

While Chavez had been fighting pesticide use since the late 1960s, growers accused him of having an ulterior motive when he enacted the boycott. In 1982 Republican George Deukmejian Jr. was elected California governor. He was backed by millions of dollars in political contributions from agribusiness. In one of his first acts, Deukmejian appointed a pro-grower lawyer to head the ALRB. By the time Chavez called the pesticide boycott, the board was barely functioning and the governor had essentially stopped enforcing California farm labor laws. For this reason, grape growers charged that Chavez's real motive was not to protect workers and consumers but to pressure the state to properly administer farm labor laws.

Whatever the motive, the Grapes of Wrath boycott was largely ineffective. Ronald Reagan, who had opposed farmworkers when he was governor, was president of the United States. Republicans were a majority in Congress, and the nation was much more conservative than it was during the Delano grape strike. Political protest was considered a thing of the past, and a 1986 study commissioned by the grape industry showed that only 5 percent of consumers were honoring the Grapes of Wrath boycott. Once again, Chavez felt the need for dramatic action to draw attention to the plight of farmworkers.

In July 1988, at the age of sixty-one, Chavez began his third hunger strike, which he called the Fast for Life. Chavez vowed to refuse solid food until growers stopped using five deadly pesticides

At a press conference in December 1987, Chavez urges people to boycott contaminated grapes.

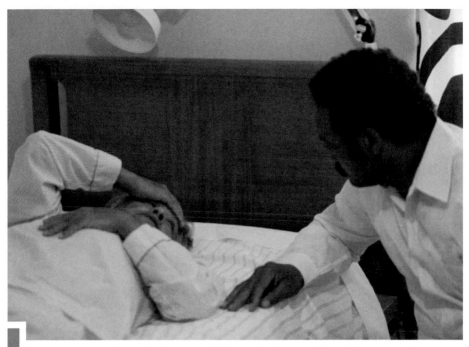

Civil rights activist the Reverend Jesse Jackson visits Chavez on the twenty-ninth day of his fast in 1988.

in their vineyards. The fast went well at first, but Chavez's health began to deteriorate rapidly during the second week. This caused great concern among his family, friends, and coworkers. Ignoring their pleas to end the fast, Chavez went thirty-six days without food. On August 21, he finally started eating again when doctors told him he was risking permanent damage to his health and possibly death.

In a scene reminiscent of earlier decades, Chavez ended his fast at a huge outdoor mass attended by celebrities, politicians, and thousands of supporters. And as before, it took Chavez months to recover. But unlike previous fasts, this one had little impact on the public. After he was strong enough to travel, Chavez felt obligated to undertake an extended speaking tour to convince consumers to boycott grapes. When he visited colleges and community centers, Chavez reminded audiences of the physical deformities seen in farmworkers' children and of the cancer clusters found in towns along Highway 99 in the Central Valley.

◼ DECREASING UNION MEMBERSHIP

As the 1980s drew to a close, all American unions, including the UFW, were struggling. Labor leaders considered Reagan one of the most antiunion presidents in U.S. history, and his administration's policies strongly favored employers over workers. This belief was backed by statistics that showed when Reagan was elected in 1980, nearly 21 percent of all American workers belonged to labor unions. At the end of his second term in 1988, that number had shrunk to 13 percent. Growing numbers of Americans viewed unions as outdated and obsolete.

While the stature of the UFW was decreasing, Chavez was increasingly seen as an elder statesmen. In 1990 the Cesar Chavez Elementary School in Coachella became the first public building to bear his name. In the years that followed, the labor leader's name would appear on dozens of other buildings, streets, and parks in U.S. cities.

Despite the honors, Chavez understood that the fight was far from over. Large numbers of illegal immigrants from Mexico were flooding into the country, taking jobs from UFW workers. Pesticides remained a problem in the fields. And agribusiness interests relentlessly fought any gains made by the union.

◼ A PLAIN PINE BOX

In April 1993, Chavez was still working on behalf of farm laborers. He was in Yuma, Arizona, to testify in court concerning the labor practices of Bruce Church Incorporated, one of the world's largest lettuce producers. Ironically, Church's vast holdings included the land where Chavez was born on his family's farm sixty-six years earlier.

In the early morning hours of April 23, Chavez died in his sleep from natural causes. He was in a hotel room only miles from the place of his birth. In the months before his death, he had told his family that he wanted a simple funeral. Respecting his wishes, his family buried Chavez in a plain pine box. State flags in California were lowered to half-mast, and forty thousand people attended the funeral, including civil rights activist Jesse Jackson and members of the Kennedy family.

Actor Edward James Olmos *(center)* and Representative Joseph Kennedy of Massachusetts *(left of center)* help carry the casket of Cesar Chavez on the half-mile (0.8 km) funeral procession in Delano in 1993.

Most attendees, however, were workers and supporters. They had fought side by side with the man who, more than anyone else, brought justice and dignity to the farmworkers of California and beyond.

"YES TO MAN'S DIGNITY"

Although Chavez was gone, the UFW continued the fight for workers' rights. Four of Chavez's eight children held prominent positions in the union, and his son-in-law, Arturo Rodriguez, took over as UFW president, a position he still held in 2010. In the years following the founder's death, the UFW has won new contracts representing workers in the rose, strawberry, wine grape, mushroom, and lettuce fields of California, Florida, and Washington.

The Grapes of Wrath boycott had mixed success before it was finally ended in 2000. While the action had little effect on pesticide use in the vineyards, it drew consumer attention to the issue. Since the early 1990s, organic food production has grown rapidly, about 20 percent a year. With millions of consumers demanding food produced without pesticides and other chemicals, growth in this sector of the food business has far outpaced the rest of the industry. Chavez was one of the first people to draw attention to the dangers of pesticide use, and since that time, the demand for organic food has turned into an international movement.

"Cesar is dead. We have wept for him
until our eyes are dry,
Dry as the fields of California that
He loved so well. . . .
Now he lies dead, and storms still rage around us.
The dispossessed walk hopeless streets,
Campesinos [farmworkers] gather
by roadside ditches to sleep,
Shrouded by pesticides, unsure of tomorrow,
Hounded by propositions that keep their children
Uneducated in a land grown fat with greed.
Yes, the arrogant hounds of hate
Are loose upon this land again, and Cesar
Weeps in the embrace of La Virgin de Guadalupe,
Still praying for his people."

—Rudolfo Anaya, from Elegy on the Death of Cesar Chavez, 2000

In the twenty-first century, organic products have risen in popularity as consumers have become willing to pay more for produce free from pesticides.

The news is less positive for those who provide the food for consumers' tables. It could be argued that farmworkers in the twenty-first century are hardly better off than those in 1970. Although the bracero program is long gone, almost half of all field-workers are undocumented immigrants, and about three-quarters of those people were born in Mexico. Six percent of the workers, about one hundred thousand, are under the age of eighteen. And by the first decade of the twenty-first century, UFW membership had dwindled to twenty-seven thousand. However, the UFW is hoping to increase its membership with the introduction of the AgJobs bill negotiated by the union and the nation's agricultural industry. This federal law would allow millions of undocumented immigrants already in the United States to become citizens. Since these people were already working in the fields, the UFW believes that the law would ensure that growers would have a legal workforce. In addition, the bill would give field hands the right to join unions and demand fair wages and better working conditions.

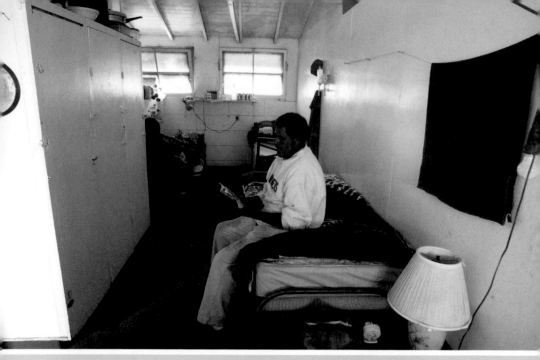

Above: A farmworker sits in a shared room at Camp Toro, which provides housing for lettuce pickers in Salinas, California, in the early 2000s. *Below:* Paul Chavez stands next to the tribute stamp for his father, Cesar Chavez, in 2003.

The success of the AgJobs bill is far from certain since many members of Congress strongly oppose citizenship for illegal immigrants. Without the protections outlined in the bill, most farmworkers would continue to live in substandard, overcrowded housing provided by growers. And pay remained at poverty levels. In the first decade of the twenty-first century, the average farmworker made ten thousand dollars a year. This meant that those who grew the food for consumers in the richest nation on Earth could barely buy enough groceries to feed their families. But the UFW continues the fight for the common workers that Chavez, Huerta, Ross, and others began in 1952.

Cesar E. Chavez's birthday has become a holiday in California and seven other states. In 2003 the U.S. Postal Service honored Chavez with a postage stamp. But Chavez would not appreciate people honoring him while forgetting the workers he sacrificed for his entire life. As he told biographer Jacques E. Levy, "Fighting for social justice ... is one of the profoundest ways in which a man can say yes to man's dignity, and that really means sacrifice. There is no way on this earth in which you can say yes to man's dignity and know that you're going to be spared some sacrifice."

1882: The U.S. government passes the Chinese Exclusion Act, preventing all immigration from China and barring Chinese people already in the United States from becoming citizens.

1907: President Theodore Roosevelt negotiates a gentlemen's agreement with Japan, which severely restricts Japanese immigration to the United States.

1913: In August the Wheatland Hop Riot erupts in Wheatland, California, killing four people and wounding six more.

1927: On March 31, Cesar Estrada Chavez is born on a small farm near Yuma, Arizona.

1937: The Chavez family is evicted from their farm. They take to the road, working as migrant laborers in California.

1948: Cesar Chavez and Helen Fabela are married. Over the years, they will have eight children.

1952: In June, Chavez meets Fred Ross and joins the Community Service Organization (CSO).

1953: Chavez is promoted to the position of statewide organizer for the CSO.

1955: Gilbert Padilla joins the CSO.

1956: Dolores Huerta joins the CSO.

1962: On March 31, Chavez resigns from the CSO so he can work full-time to build the National Farm Workers Association (NFWA). On September 30, the NFWA holds its first convention at an abandoned theater in Fresno.

1965: On September 8, Filipino vineyard workers begin the Delano grape strike backed by their union, the Agricultural Workers Organizing Committee (AWOC). On September 16, NFWA joins the strike.

1966: In March and April, strikers from NFWA and AWOC march 250 miles (402 km) from Delano to Sacramento to publicize the boycott against Schenley Industries. In July the two unions merge to form the United Farm Workers Organizing Committee (UFWOC).

1967: UFWOC begins a national boycott of Giumarra, the world's largest grower of table grapes.

1968: In February, after strikers threaten violence against growers, Chavez undertakes a hunger strike to bring the movement to a halt. In June, New York senator and UFWOC supporter Senator Robert F. Kennedy is assassinated in Los Angeles.

1970: UFWOC signs a contract with Delano grape growers, bringing an end to the strike and boycott.

1972: UFWOC is affiliated with the AFL-CIO and changes its name to the United Farm Workers of America (UFW). Chavez fasts in Arizona to protest a restrictive farm labor law.

1973: California grape growers refuse to renew their UFWOC contracts and sign with the Teamsters instead.

1975: The California legislature passes the Agriculture Labor Relations Act, the first law recognizing the rights of farmworkers.

1984: Chavez begins the Grapes of Wrath boycott to protest the use of cancer-causing pesticides in the vineyards.

1988: Chavez conducts the thirty-six-day Fast for Life to draw attention to the grape boycott.

1993: Chavez dies in Yuma, Arizona. His funeral in Delano is attended by forty thousand people.

2000: The Grapes of Wrath boycott is ended.

2003: The Cesar E. Chavez commemorative stamp is issued by the U.S. Postal Service.

2005: The UFW concludes a successful campaign against the Gallo winery that results in a new workers' contract.

2010: UFW leaders and members join thousands in a rally in Las Vegas, Nevada, to press for U.S. government reform of immigration laws.

Cesar Chavez

(1927–1993) Chavez was a Mexican American farmworker born near Yuma, Arizona. He became a community organizer, civil rights activist, and labor leader. In 1952 he took a job with the Community Service Organization (CSO) registering voters and helping migrant workers with their struggles against injustice. Chavez formed the National Farm Workers Association (NFWA) in 1962, a group that helped with the Delano grape strike in 1965. In 1966 the NFWA merged with another union to form the United Farm Workers Organizing Committee (UFWOC). Chavez was executive director of this union when it won the grape strike in 1970. In the following years, he saw his creation, now called the United Farm Workers (UFW), organize strikes and boycotts to get higher wages from produce growers. During the 1980s, he led a boycott to protest the use of toxic pesticides. Chavez's birthday is a state holiday in California and seven other states.

Dolores Huerta

(b. 1930) Huerta was born in Dawson, New Mexico. She is the cofounder and first vice president emeritus of the United Farm Workers of America. Huerta joined the Community Service Organization in 1956 and broke gender barriers working as a community organizer and lobbyist in Sacramento and Washington, D.C. She quit the CSO in 1962 to cofound the National Farm Workers Association with Chavez. Huerta played an important role in the Delano grape strike, negotiating contracts, directing boycotts, and lobbying politicians. Over the years, Huerta has been arrested twenty-two times for participating in nonviolent civil disobedience activities and strikes. In 2010, at the age of eighty, she was the president of the Dolores Huerta Foundation, an organization dedicated to working for equal access to health care, housing, education, and jobs for those in disadvantaged communities, with an emphasis on serving women and children.

Larry D. Itliong

(1913–1977) Born in the Philippines, Larry Itliong moved to the United States at the age of sixteen and worked first in Alaska gold mines and later in California farm fields. Itliong cofounded the Filipino Farm Labor Union in California in 1956 and the Agricultural Workers Organizing Committee (AWOC) in 1959. He was instrumental in calling the Delano grape strike, and in 1967, he became assistant director to Cesar Chavez in the United Farm Workers Organizing Committee. Itliong quit the UFW in 1971 and dedicated the rest of his life to a variety of community and civic projects aimed at improving the lives of Filipino farmworkers.

Robert F. Kennedy

(1925–1968) Kennedy, born in Brookline, Massachusetts, was the brother of President John F. Kennedy. He was the U.S. attorney general from 1961 to 1964 and was elected a U.S. senator from New York in 1965. In 1966 Kennedy was a prominent member of the U.S. Senate Subcommittee on Migratory Labor that met in Delano to investigate the living and working conditions of farm laborers. While in Delano, he joined Chavez and other strikers to walk the picket line at DiGiorgio Fruit Corporation's ranch. In the following years, Kennedy introduced Chavez to influential leaders in Washington, D.C., and New York. Kennedy was assassinated in Los Angeles after winning the California presidential primary in June 1968.

Eugene Nelson

(1929–1999) Nelson was an author and labor leader. He was born on a ranch in Modesto, California, and worked thinning sugar beets with Mexican American field hands during his high school years. Nelson moved to Delano in the early 1960s to join the NFWA. He was part of the association when the grape strike began in 1965 and served as a picket captain during the first days of the labor action. In 1966 he published *Huelga*, his eyewitness account of the first one hundred days of the Delano grape strike. That same year, he also became the Texas director of the national grape boycott. In later years, Nelson joined the Industrial Workers of the World (Wobblies) and worked as an advocate for farmworkers.

Gilbert Padilla

(b. 1928) Padilla was born in a labor camp near Los Banos, California. He became a volunteer in the Community Service Organization beginning in 1955. In 1960 he was hired as a staff member by Cesar Chavez. He quit in 1962 and became codirector of the National Farm Workers Association. In 1965 Padilla worked for the California Migrant Ministry, where he played a central role in the Woodville and Linnell rent strikes. During the Delano grape strike, Padilla was one of Chavez's closest associates. He helped with the Schenley and DiGiorgio boycotts. Padilla was elected secretary-treasurer of the UFW in 1973 and worked closely with Chavez until Padilla retired from the organization in 1977.

Fred Ross

(1910–1992) Ross was a political activist who founded the Community Service Organization (CSO) in 1948. Ross was a San Francisco native who worked for the federal government managing migrant labor camps for the Farm Services Administration during the Depression. After World War II, he started the CSO when he witnessed discrimination, police brutality, and poor housing in Mexican American neighborhoods. In the 1950s, he recruited and trained Cesar Chavez and Dolores Huerta and promoted them through the ranks of the CSO. In the early 1960s, Ross left the CSO and worked through the National Presbyterian Church to help destitute Yaqui Indians in southern Arizona. In the 1970s, Ross rejoined Chavez and helped train a new generation of leaders for the UFW, where he worked until the early 1980s.

Luis Valdez

(b. 1940) Valdez, a writer and director, has been described as the father of Chicano theater and cinema. Valdez, one of ten children in a family of farmworkers, lived in Delano and began working in the fields as a child. He was the first member of his family to attend college, studying theater and drama at San Jose State University in the early 1960s. When the Delano grape strike began, Valdez returned to Delano to work with the NFWA. He founded El Teatro Campesino (the Farmworkers Theater) in 1965 to teach social, political, and economic lessons through humorous and dramatic skits. After the strike ended, Valdez taught drama at the University of California at Berkeley and Santa Cruz from 1971 to 1974. Since that time, Valdez has served on the advisory boards at KCET public television in Los Angeles and the National Endowment for the Arts. He also wrote and directed the Broadway play Zoot Suit, which was made into a film in 1981.

Philip Vera Cruz

(1904–1994) Vera Cruz was a Filipino immigrant who moved to the United States in 1926, where he faced racial discrimination and oppressive labor practices. In 1959 he cofounded the Agricultural Workers Organizing Committee (AWOC) to fight for the rights of Filipino farmworkers. In 1965 Vera Cruz was active in calling the Delano grape strike. In the early days of the strike, he helped organize sit-ins at labor camps and picket lines at ranches. He also helped convince NFWA leaders to join forces with AWOC. When the two unions merged into UFWOC, Vera Cruz served as vice president and the highest-ranking Filipino officer. He resigned from the UFW in 1977 but remained active in union and social justice causes.

activist: someone who works toward achieving political or social goals

agribusiness: operations and businesses that are associated with large-scale farming

blacklist: a list of people who are shunned as employees because they have engaged in union organizing or other activities deemed undesirable

boycott: a means of protest in which consumers refuse to buy a company's products because of its politics or policies

bracero: a Mexican worker recruited to perform farmwork in the United States as part of the bracero program operated by the U.S. federal government between 1942 and 1964

cannery: a place where fruits, vegetables, or other foods are packaged into cans

Cold War: a phrase used to describe the intense rivalry and hostility between the United States and the Soviet Union that developed after World War II and ended with the collapse of the Soviet Union in 1991

Communism: a system of government based on the belief that the wealth and resources of a nation belong equally to all of its citizens

immigrant: someone who has entered the country from another country and permanently resides there; immigrants are often fleeing poverty, discrimination, or warfare in their homelands

migrant: someone who travels from one region to another in search of work

naturalization: the process of becoming a U.S. citizen

registrar: a public official whose duties include registering voters

scab: a term for a person who works in defiance of a strike; a strikebreaker

union: an organization of working people set up to advance its members' interests in terms of wages, working hours, and other conditions

5 United Farm Workers, "The Rise of the UFW," UFW History, 2006, http://www.ufw.org/_page.php?menu =research&inc=history/03 .html (November 17, 2009).

6 Susan Ferris and Ricardo Sandoval, *The Fight in the Fields: Cesar Chavez and the Farmworkers Movement* (New York: Harcourt Brace & Company, 1997), 87.

6 United Farm Workers, "The Rise of the UFW."

6 Eugene Nelson, *Huelga* (Delano, CA: Farm Worker Press, 1966), 22.

8 Ibid., 15.

10 Cletus E. Daniel, *Bitter Harvest* (Ithaca, NY: Cornell University Press, 1981), 21.

12 *Revolutionary Worker*, "Sacramento Delta Blues," February 16, 1997, n.d., http://rwor.org/a/ firstvol/890-899/894/chines .htm (November 17, 2009).

13 Ibid.

13 Ibid.

14 Daniel, *Bitter Harvest*, 35.

15 Sam Kushner, *Long Road to Delano* (New York: International Publishers, 1975), 13.

16 Eldon R. Penrose, *California Nativism: Organized Opposition to the Japanese, 1890–1930* (San Francisco: R and E Research Associates, 1973), 76.

21 Mark Leier, *Where the Fraser River Flows: The Industrial Workers of the World in British Columbia* (Vancouver, BC: New Star Books, 1990), 35.

21 Daniel, *Bitter Harvest*, 90.

22 Linda C. Majka and Theo J. Majka, *Farm Workers, Agribusiness, and the State* (Philadelphia: Temple University, 1982), 54.

23 Kushner, *Long Road to Delano*, 18.

23–24 Stuart Marshall Jamieson, *Labor Unionism in American Agriculture* (Washington, DC: U.S. Department of Labor, 1946), 74.

25 Kushner, *Long Road to Delano*, 16.

26 Ibid.

28 Kitty Calavita, *Inside the State.* (New York: Routledge, 1992), 1.

29 Ibid., 32.

30 Richard W. Etulain, ed. *César Chávez: A Brief Biography with Documents* (Boston: Bedford/St. Martins, 2002), 3.

32 Ferris and Sandoval, *The Fight in the Fields*, 26.

32 Ibid., 13.

33 Jacques E. Levy, *Cesar Chavez: Autobiography of La Causa* (New York: W. W. Norton & Company, 1975), 74–75.

34 Ibid., 92.

36 Ibid., 99.

36 Ronald B. Taylor, *Chavez and the Farm Workers* (Boston: Beacon Press, 1975), 83.

38 Richard Griswold del Castillo and Richard A. Garcia, *César Chávez: A Triumph of Spirit* (Norman: University of Oklahoma Press, 1995), 27.

39 Etulain, *César Chávez: A Brief Biography with Documents*, 32.

40–41 Ibid., 39–40.

42 Jacques E. Levy, *Cesar Chavez*, 129.

43 Ernesto Galarza, *Farm Workers and Agri-Business in California, 1947–1960* (Notre Dame, IN: University of Notre Dame Press, 1977), 251–252.

46 Ferris and Sandoval, *The Fight in the Fields*, 61.

46–47 Griswold del Castillo and

Garcia, *César Chávez*, 64.

47   Etulain, *César Chávez*, 40.

48   Cesar Chavez, "Editorial: Enough People with One Idea," *El Malcriado*, no. 19, Farmworker Movement Archives, n.d., http://www.farmworkermovement.us/ufwarchives/elmalcriado/adair/No19.pdf (March 26, 2009).

48–49   Jacques E. Levy, *Cesar Chavez*, 163.

50   Francisco Arturo Rosales, *Chicano!* (Houston: Arte Publico Press, 1997), 144.

51   Jacques E. Levy, *Cesar Chavez*, 173.

52   Gilbert Padilla, "Gilbert Padilla 1962–1980," Farmworker Movement Archives, n.d., http://farmworkermovement.com/essays/essays/005%20Padilla_Gilbert.pdf (November 12, 2009).

53   Dolores Huerta, "Her Second Wind," Dolores Huerta Foundation, n.d., http://dhuerta.hostcentric.com/dh_bio.htm (November 17, 2009).

54   Ferris and Sandoval, *The Fight in the Fields*, 77.

56   Kushner, *Long Road to Delano*, 115.

58   Andy Zermeno, *Don Sotaco: Cartoons from the Delano Grape Strike* (Delano, CA: Farm Worker Press, 1966), 4.

58   Ibid., 4.

60–61   Ferris and Sandoval, *The Fight in the Fields*, 86.

61–62   Jacques E. Levy, *Cesar Chavez*, 183.

62   Cesar Chavez, *El Malcriado*, no. 19.

62–63   Nelson, *Huelga*, 21.

64   Jack London, "Definition of a Strikebreaker," Farmworker Movement Archives, n.d., http://www.farmworkermovement.org/essays/essays/Jack%20London%20-%20Definition%20of%20Strikebreaker.pdf (March 27, 2009).

64   Nelson, *Huelga*, 26.

64   Ibid.

65   Ibid., 31.

65   Jacques E. Levy, *Cesar Chavez*, 184.

67   *El Macriado*, no. 22, Farmworker Movement Archives, n.d., http://www.farmworkermovement.us/ufwarchives/elmalcriado/SFSU/No_Date_No_22.pdf (May 15, 2009).

68   *El Malcriado*, "Radovich sprays 16 strikers with Blinding Sulfur," no. 21, Farmworker Movement Archives, n.d., http://farmworkermovement.com/ufwarchives/elmalcriado/adair/No21.pdf (March 28, 2009).

68   Jacques E. Levy, *Cesar Chavez*, 195–196.

71   John C. Hammerback and Richard J. Jensen, *The Rhetorical Career of Cesar Chavez* (College Station: Texas A&M University Press, 2003), 70.

72   *El Malcriado*, "The Plan of Delano," no. 33, Farmworker Movement Archives, n.d., http://www.farmworkermovement.us/ufwarchives/elmalcriado/1966/April%2010,%201966.pdf (April 13, 2010).

74   "Boycott Instructions–Delano Grapes/Schenley Liquors 1966," Farmworker Movement Archives, n.d., http://www.farmworkermovement.us/essays/essays/MillerArchive/012A%20Boycott%20Instructions.pdf (March 29, 2009).

78 Ferris and Sandoval, *The Fight in the Fields*, 119.

78–79 Richard J. Jensen and John C. Hammerback, eds. *The Words of César Chávez* (College Station: Texas A&M University Press, 2002), 18.

80 Ferris and Sandoval, *The Fight in the Fields*, 115–116.

80–81 Kushner, *Long Road to Delano*, 164–165.

81 Steven W. Bender, *One Night in America: Robert Kennedy, César Chávez, and the Dream of Dignity* (Boulder, CO: Paradigm Publishers, 2008), 26.

82 Jacques E. Levy, *Cesar Chavez*, 209.

84 Ibid., 210.

85 Ibid., 212.

87 Ferris and Sandoval, *The Fight in the Fields*, 126.

90 Jacques E. Levy, *Cesar Chavez*, 227.

91 Dick Meister and Anne Loftis, *A Long Time Coming: The Struggle to Unionize America's Farm Workers* (New York: Macmillan Publishing, 1977), 151.

92 Jacques E. Levy, *Cesar Chavez*, 267.

94 Griswold del Castillo and Garcia, *Cesar Chavez*, 94.

95 Peter B. Levy, *America in the Sixties Right, Left, and Center* (Westport, CT: Praeger, 1998), 92.

97 Bender, *One Night in America*, 69.

97 Jacques E. Levy, *Cesar Chavez*, 272.

98 Ibid., 273.

99 Taylor, *Chavez*, 223.

100 Ibid., 224.

100–101 Bender, *One Night in America*, 156–157.

101 Hammerback and Jensen, *The Rhetorical Career*, 116.

103 Robert F. Kennedy, "Robert F. Kennedy Speech," The History Place, n.d., http://www.historyplace.com/speeches/rfk.htm (November 17, 2009).

104 Cesar Chavez, El Macriado, 1, no. 4, Farmworker Movement Archives, n.d., http://www.farmworkermovement.us/ufwarchives/index.shtml#malcriado (March 28, 2009).

106 Taylor, *Chavez*, 234.

107 Ibid., 230.

108 Ibid., 232.

109 Ibid., 237.

115 Ibid., 217.

115 Ferris and Sandoval, *The Fight in the Fields*, 157.

116 Etulain, *César Chávez*, 115.

119 Jensen and Hammerback, *The Words of César Chávez*, 47.

120 Ibid.

124 Ilan Stavans, ed., *Cesar Chavez: An Organizer's Tale* (New York: Penguin Books, 2008), 137.

125 Ibid., 136.

127–128 Agricultural Labor Relations Board, State of California, 2007, http://www.alrb.ca.gov (April 13, 2010).

129 Ferris and Sandoval, *The Fight in the Fields*, 209.

129–130 Craig Scharlin and Lilia V. Villanueva. *Philip Vera Cruz* (Seattle: University of Washington Press, 2000), 113.

130 Ibid., 115–116.

136 Diana Hembree, ed., *The Fight in the Fields: Cesar Chavez and the Farmworkers Movement* (New York: Harcourt Brace & Company, 1997), 266.

139 Jacques E. Levy, *Cesar Chavez*, 539.

Bender, Steven W. *One Night in America: Robert Kennedy, César Chávez, and the Dream of Dignity.* Boulder, CO: Paradigm Publishers, 2008.

"Boycott Instructions–Delano Grapes/Schenley Liquors 1966." Farm Workers Movement. N.d. http://www.farmworkermovement.us/essays/essays/MillerArchive/012A%20Boycott%20Instructions.pdf (March 29, 2009).

Calavita, Kitty. *Inside the State.* New York: Routledge, 1992.

Chavez, Cesar. "Editorial: Enough People with One Idea." *El Malcriado,* no. 19. Farmworker Movement Archives. N.d. http://www.farmworkermovement.us/ufwarchives/elmalcriado/adair/No19.pdf (March 26, 2009).

Daniel, Cletus E. *Bitter Harvest.* Ithaca, NY: Cornell University Press, 1981.

Etulain, Richard W., ed. *César Chávez: A Brief Biography with Documents.* Boston: Bedford/St. Martins, 2002.

Ferris, Susan, and Ricardo Sandoval. *The Fight in the Fields: Cesar Chavez and the Farmworkers Movement.* New York: Harcourt Brace & Company, 1997.

Galarza, Ernesto. *Farm Workers and Agri-Business in California, 1947–1960.* Notre Dame, IN: University of Notre Dame Press, 1977.

Griswold del Castillo, Richard, and Richard A. Garcia. *César Chávez: A Triumph of Spirit.* Norman: University of Oklahoma Press, 1995.

Guthrie, Woody. "(If You Ain't Got the) Do Re Mi." Transcribed by Manfred Helfert. N.d. http://www.woodyguthrie.de/doremi.html (November 17, 2008).

Hammerback, John C., and Richard J. Jensen. *The Rhetorical Career of Cesar Chavez.* College Station: Texas A&M University Press, 2003.

Hembree, Diana, ed. *The Fight in the Fields: Cesar Chavez and the Farmworkers Movement.* New York: Harcourt Brace & Company, 1997.

Huerta, Dolores. "Her Second Wind." Dolores Huerta Foundation. N.d. http://dhuerta.hostcentric.com/dh_bio.htm (November 17, 2009).

Jamieson, Stuart Marshall. *Labor Unionism in American Agriculture.* Washington, DC: U.S. Department of Labor, 1946.

Jensen, Richard J., and John C. Hammerback, eds. *The Words of César Chávez.* College Station: Texas A&M University Press, 2002.

Kennedy, Robert F. "Robert F. Kennedy Speech." The History Place. N.d. http://www.historyplace.com/speeches/rfk.htm (November 17, 2009).

Kushner, Sam. *Long Road to Delano.* New York: International Publishers, 1975.

Leier, Mark. *Where the Fraser River Flows: The Industrial Workers of the World in British Columbia.* Vancouver, BC: New Star Books, 1990.

Levy, Jacques E. *Cesar Chavez: Autobiography of La Causa*. New York: W. W. Norton & Company, 1975.

Levy, Peter B. *America in the Sixties Right, Left, and Center*. Westport, CT: Praeger, 1998.

London, Jack. "Definition of a Strikebreaker." Farmworker Movement Archives. N.d. http://www.farmworkermovement.org/essays/essays/Jack%20London%20 -%20Definition%20of%20Strikebreaker.pdf (March 27, 2009).

Majka, Linda C., and Theo J. Majka. *Farm Workers, Agribusiness, and the State*. Philadelphia: Temple University, 1982.

Meister, Dick, and Anne Loftis. *A Long Time Coming: The Struggle to Unionize America's Farm Workers*. New York: Macmillan Publishing, 1977.

Nelson, Eugene. *Huelga*. Delano, CA: Farm Worker Press, 1966.

Penrose, Eldon R. *California Nativism: Organized Opposition to the Japanese, 1890–1930*. San Francisco: R and E Research Associates, 1973.

Revolutionary Worker. "Sacramento Delta Blues." February 16, 1997. N.d. http://rwor .org/a/firstvol/890-899/894/chines.htm (November 17, 2009).

Rosales, Francisco Arturo. *Chicano!* Houston: Arte Publico Press, 1997.

Scharlin, Craig, and Lilia V. Villanueva. *Philip Vera Cruz*. Seattle: University of Washington Press, 2000.

Stavans, Ilan, ed. *Cesar Chavez: An Organizer's Tale*. New York: Penguin Books, 2008.

Taylor, Ronald B. *Chavez*. Boston: Beacon Press, 1975.

United Farm Workers. "The Rise of the UFW." UFW History. 2006. http://www .ufw.org/_page.php?menu=research&inc=history/03.htm (November 17, 2009).

Zermeno, Andy. *Don Sotaco: Cartoons from the Delano Grape Strike*. Delano, CA: Farm Worker Press, 1966.

Behnke, Alison. *Mexicans in America*. Minneapolis: Lerner Publications Company, 2005. The book examines the history of Mexican immigration to the United States, discussing why Mexicans move to the United States, what their lives are like after they arrive, where they settle, and customs they bring from home.

Collins, David R. *Cesar Chavez*. Minneapolis: Lerner Publications Company, 2005. A biography of the leader of the Delano grape strike details his childhood and the difficulties he surmounted to gain equality for farmworkers.

Cooper, Michael L. *Dust to Eat: Drought and Depression in the 1930's*. New York: Clarion Books, 2004. A trip through Depression-era America chronicles the everyday struggle of those who lost everything before heading to California to seek work in the fields and orchards.

Frank, Sarah. *Filipinos in America*. Minneapolis: Lerner Publications Company, 2006. The story of Filipinos in the United States, the prejudices they faced, their struggles for equality, and their contributions to American culture are outlined in this book.

Manheimer, Ann. *Martin Luther King Jr.* Minneapolis: Twenty-First Century Books, 2005. This biography of the famed civil rights leader includes his childhood in Atlanta, his rise to power and influence, and his tragic death.

Nahmias, Rick. *The Migrant Project: Contemporary California Farm Workers*. Albuquerque: University of New Mexico Press, 2008. This book contains essays, eyewitness accounts, and oral histories by migrant workers, civil rights lawyers, and others, including Dolores Huerta and José R. Padilla, who fought for equal rights in the fields.

Sanna, Ellyn. *Mexican Americans' Role in the United States: A History of Pride, a Future of Hope*. Philadelphia: Mason Crest Publishers, 2006. This book explores the history and culture of Latino Americans and how are they contributing to the United States' growth and culture.

Skurzynski, Gloria. *Sweat and Blood*. Minneapolis: Twenty-First Century Books, 2009. This history of U.S. labor unions traces them from colonial times through industrialization in the twentieth century and into the modern era.

Soto, Gary. *Jessie De La Cruz: A Profile of a United Farm Worker*. New York: Persea Books, 2000. The inspiring story of Jessie De La Cruz, field-worker at the age of five who joined the fledgling United Farm Workers union, became its first woman recruiter, participated in strikes, and testified before the Senate.

Street, Richard Steven. *Everyone Had Cameras: Photography and Farmworkers in California, 1850–2000*. Minneapolis: University of Minnesota Press, 2008. A history of American photography as it was used to document images of workers in the fields from the nineteenth century through the Great Depression and into the present.

Worth Richard. *Dolores Huerta*. New York: Chelsea House, 2008. The book follows the cofounder of the National Farm Workers Association as she organizes strikes, marches, and demonstrations, and negotiates contracts with powerful growers on behalf of the UFW.

Websites

Cesar Chavez Foundation
> http://www.chavezfoundation.org
> This foundation was created in 1993 by the Chavez family to educate people about the life and work of the civil rights leader and to inspire people to carry on his values and vision for a better world. The foundation supports educational programs, service clubs, and youth action programs.

Cultivating Creativity: The Arts and the Farm Workers' Movement during the 1960s and '70s
> http://www.library.sfsu.edu/exhibits/cultivating/default.html
> There were many creative forces active during the early years of the NFWA, and this site contains links to photos, songs, and drawings from the Delano grape strike.

Farmworker Movement Documentation Project
> http://www.farmworkermovement.us/ufwarchives/index.shtml#malcriado
> This site contains important documents relating to the NFWA and the UFW, with links to Cesar Chavez's writings, his FBI file, newspaper articles about the Delano strike, and every issue of *El Malcriado* ever published.

Industrial Workers of the World
> http://www.iww.org
> The official website of the Industrial Workers of the World, or Wobblies, contains events, news, history, and other information that relates to worker rights in Europe, the United States, Australia, and elsewhere.

National Farm Worker Ministry
> http://www.nfwm.org
> This is the website of the interfaith organization that supports farmworkers as they organize for justice and equality. The site provides news, action alerts, history, and information about ongoing projects.

United Farm Workers
> http://www.ufw.org
> The official website of the UFW contains historic photos from the Delano grape strike, information about Cesar Chavez, an events calendar, and reports on current issues facing farmworkers.

PHOTO ACKNOWLEDGMENTS

The images in this book are used with the permission of: Walter P. Reuther Library, Wayne State University, pp. 5, 19 (both), 31, 33, 37, 41, 46, 49, 50, 55, 128; © Arthur Schatz/Time & Life Pictures/Getty Images, pp. 7, 105; AP Photo/RCA Victor, p. 9; © Laura Westlund/Independent Picture Service, p. 11; © Huntington Library/SuperStock, p. 12; © Buyenlarge/Hulton Archive/Getty Images, pp. 14, 24–25; © Science and Society/SuperStock, p. 22; Walter P. Reuther Library, Wayne State University, photographer Cris Sanchez, pp. 25, 123 (top); National Archives, p. 27 (210-62-C153); AP Photo, pp. 28–29, 39, 56, 79, 83, 100, 112, 114, 119, 123 (bottom), 124; © DPA/The Image Works, p. 35; © 1976 George Ballis/Take Stock/ The Image Works, pp. 54, 64, 66, 68–69, 81, 89; Walter P. Reuther Library, Wayne State University, photographer John A. Kouns, p. 59; © Ted Streshinsky/CORBIS, pp. 70, 84, 92; © Wesley Boxce/Liaison/Getty Images, p. 75; © Bettmann/CORBIS, pp. 76, 96 (both), 121; AP Photo/Walter Zeboski, pp. 86, 87; © 1976 Bob Fitch/ Take Stock/The Image Works, pp. 91, 127; Walter P. Reuther Library, Wayne State University, photographer Dick Darby, pp. 101, 102; Walter P. Reuther Library, Wayne State University, photographer The Hamilton Spectator, pp. 106–107; © Eriss/Pix Inc./Time & Life Pictures/Getty Images, p. 111; AP Photo/Harold Filan, p. 113; © Jeff Franko/Bettmann/CORBIS, p. 132; AP Photo/Paul Sakuma, p. 133; AP Photo/Bob Galbraith, pp. 134–135; AP Photo/Stephan Savoia, p. 137; © Ted Soqui/CORBIS, p. 138 (top); AP Photo/Nick Ut, p. 138 (bottom).

Front cover: © 1976 George Ballis/Take Stock/The Image Works.

ABOUT THE AUTHOR

Stuart A. Kallen has written more than two hundred and fifty nonfiction books for children and young adults over the past twenty years. His books have covered countless aspects of human history, culture, and science, from the building of the pyramids to the music of the twenty-first century. Some of his recent titles include Open the Jail Doors—We Want to Enter, The Sandinista Revolution, Postmodern Art, and Harlem Renaissance. Kallen, who lives in San Diego, California, is also a singer-songwriter and a guitarist.